# Why the Adirondacks Look the way They do

## A Natural History
by Mike Storey

Text, photos and illustrations copyright 2006 by Mike Storey, except as noted
Self-Published by Mike Storey. First Edition 2006

Copyright 2006 by Mike Storey. No portion of this material may be reproduced in any form by any process without written permission of the author.

Cover Design by Mike Storey

Editing by Phil Brown

Desk Top Publishing by Sue Bibeau.


Printed in the United States of America by Hamilton Printing Company
10 9 8 7 6 5 4 3 2 1


Library of Congress Catalog-in-Publication Data

Storey, Mike
     Why the Adirondacks Look the Way They Do: a natural history / Mike Storey. Photographs and illustrations by the author. 1st Edition
     p.   cm.
     Includes glossary of ecological terms and index.
     ISBN 0-9777172-0-8
1. Adirondack Park—New York State  2. Natural History  3. Ecology of New York State  I. Title

QK        2006
582.
2006
CIP

# Why the **Adirondacks** Look the way They do

## A Natural History
by Mike Storey

**With Photos and Illustrations by the Author**

*To my wife, Joan, my best friend and companion in life. Thanks for being with me through the good, as well as the tough times. We sure can laugh together.
And to Tom, our son, whose love of the Adirondacks brings us joy.*

# Thanks!

Many talented and inspiring folks played a role in this book. My retired college professors from the SUNY College of Environmental Science and Forestry, Dr. David Hanselman and Dr. Edwin Ketchledge, gave me the tools, knowledge and communication skills to delve into this work. The late state geologist, Ingvar Isachsen, helped me to understand and teach the complex geology of the Adirondack region so that lay people might better understand it.

My friend, Dick Beamish, publisher of the *Adirondack Explorer,* has championed the preservation of the Adirondacks through thoughtful editorial philosophy and relentless search for citizen knowledge that empowers wise environmental decision-making. Keep up the good work! And Clarence Petty and the late Greenie Chase, whose insightful love and understanding of the Adirondack landscape opened my eyes to the magic of this place. Paul Wilbur, pilot, and overseer of Speculator's Sacandaga Pathway Nature Trail, allowed me to get many of the aerial photos used in these pages. Thanks for your friendship, Paul.

Finch Pruyn and Co. of Glens Falls, generously gave at cost the paper for the first printing of this book; it is fitting that it is printed on paper made from Adirondack wood fiber!

The self-publication of this book was made possible with the editorial mastery of Phil Brown and the desk-top publishing skills of Sue Bibeau. Critical grammatical advice and prodding to finish this book was cheerfully offered by my wife, Joan. Many thanks to you all.

# Contents

**Introduction**   1

**Chapter 1.** Modern Mountains from Ancient Rock   3

**Chapter 2.** The Age of Ice   35

**Chapter 3.** The Great North Woods   65

**Chapter 4.** Reading the Landscape   103

**Glossary of Ecological Terms**   155

**Index**   161

# Introduction

Why do the Adirondacks look the way they do? This was a question that kept popping up as my fellow naturalists at the Adirondack Park Agency's Visitor Interpretive Center at Paul Smiths tried to formulate a new plan for the center's main exhibit room. After speaking with thousands of visitors over the years, we knew that people had many questions about the natural history of the Adirondacks, as well as many misconceptions. My quarter-century as a naturalist for the APA took me to every corner of the Adirondacks, answering countless questions of school children, tourists, and college students. My experiences inspired me to write this book. The Adirondack Park is a fascinating place that demands a new look at how the landscape came to be and how nature operates in this magnificent place.

I've used the word Adirondacks as a plural to encompass this jumble of mountains, with its rivers, lakes, forests and wildlife as an ecological unit. The Adirondack Park is a political entity that was created in 1892 by the people of New York State. The Park boundary incorporates just about all (six million acres) of the ecological setting that nature exhibits as the Adirondack region.

The ecological fabric of the Adirondacks is built upon the geological foundation, and we'll explore how the geology controls the region's landscape and life. The book is also about change—sometimes astonishingly fast, sometimes imperceptibly slow—and how understanding these forces helps you comprehend why the Adirondacks look the way they do.

The human spirit suffers without the direct contact with the natural world. Here in the Adirondacks, that contact is easy and inevitable. Rachel Carson noted that, "Those who dwell, as scientists or layman, among the beauties and mysteries of the earth are never alone or weary of life." The Adirondack Park awaits your reading of its landscape to learn "Why the Adirondacks look the way they do."

**2    Why the Adirondacks Look the Way They Do**

# Chapter 1   Modern Mountains from Ancient Rock

The Adirondacks are the youngest mountains in the eastern United States, and they're still growing! They are merely adolescent in age but look old, for several reasons. First, the Adirondacks are made of billion-year-old rock, the buried roots of an ancient mountain range worn down eons ago, then about 10 million years ago, uplifted in a process that continues today. Second, the Adirondacks were overrun by four continental ice sheets two miles thick during the past million and a half years. The scouring ice ground down the peaks and widened the valleys and, when it melted, left the landscape pockmarked and choked with sand and

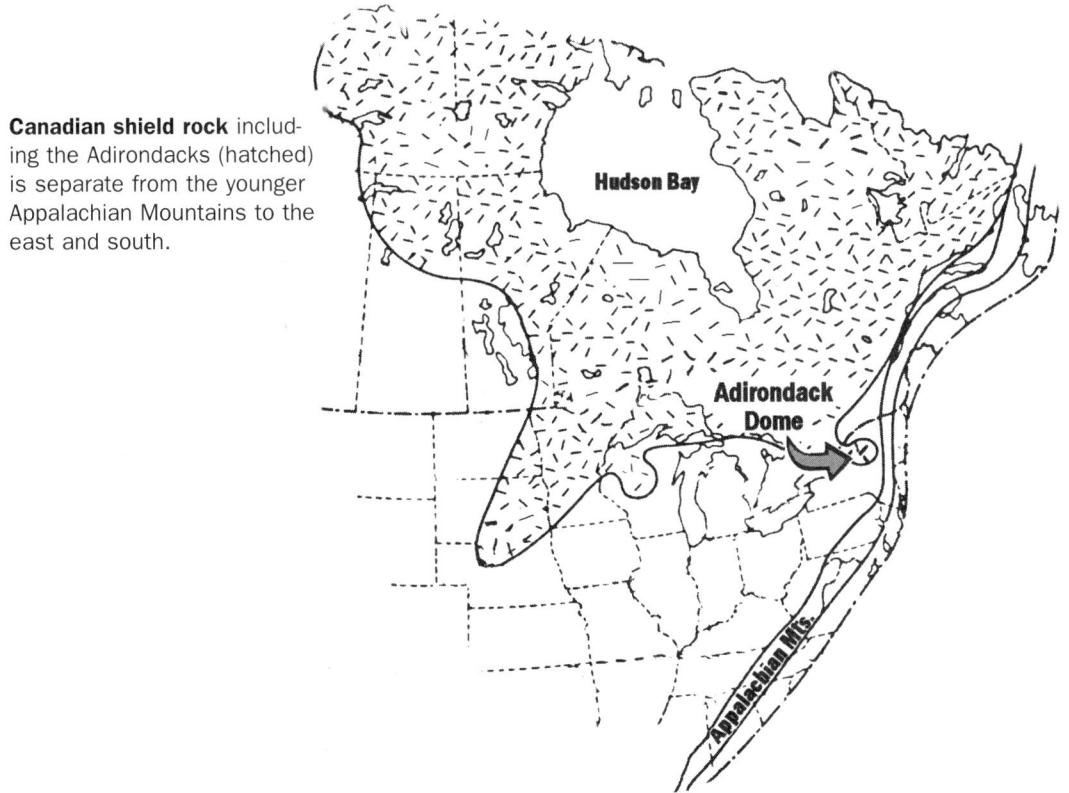

**Canadian shield rock** including the Adirondacks (hatched) is separate from the younger Appalachian Mountains to the east and south.

gravel. This sequence of geological events molded the Adirondack landscape. But there is far more to the story that we need to explore to truly understand why the Adirondacks look the way they do.

To understand the landscape, we have to travel back in time nearly half the age of the earth, some two billion years ago, when blue-green algae was the only life on earth and when some of the rock now at the surface was just a soft ooze at the bottom of an ancient sea. The Adirondacks are connected geologically to the Canadian Shield, the ancient basement rock that undergirds the North American continent. The Thousand Islands of the St. Lawrence River are located where this tough rock that connects the Adirondacks to Canada is exposed.

The bedrock now at the surface in the Adirondacks was created during a great continental collision 1.1 billion years ago. At that time, this region was located on a submerged continental shelf, similar to that off the East Coast today. The Adirondack region of then was just about at the Equator and rotated 90 degrees clockwise. Sediments had built to a depth of 50,000 feet in the shelf. When a continent-size chunk of the crust collided with proto-North America, the sea-floor sediments were pushed deep below this continent and pressure-cooked for nearly half a billion

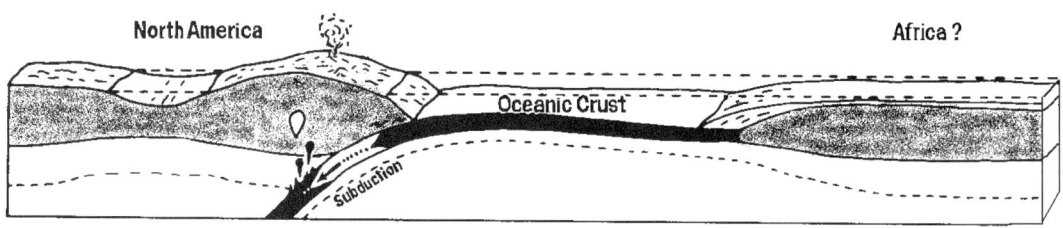

**The beginning of the Grenville Orogeny**, about 1.3 billion years ago. During this time, the ancestral Atlantic Ocean closed and the sea floor was pushed beneath North America, where it was heated and melted. Mountains above were uplifted and intruded by molten rock. A complex mixture of rocks was created in the root zone—the rocks now found at the surface of today's Adirondacks.

# Modern Mountains from Ancient Rocks 5

**Continental plates**, about 225 million years ago. From this position, North America drifted "northwest," Antarctica "south." The Indian plate headed on a long journey toward the Asian plate. The Himalayas were thrust up in that collision many millions of years later. As the Atlantic Ocean opened, it split the eastern shore of North America unevenly, stranding rock types that now are also found in western Scotland.

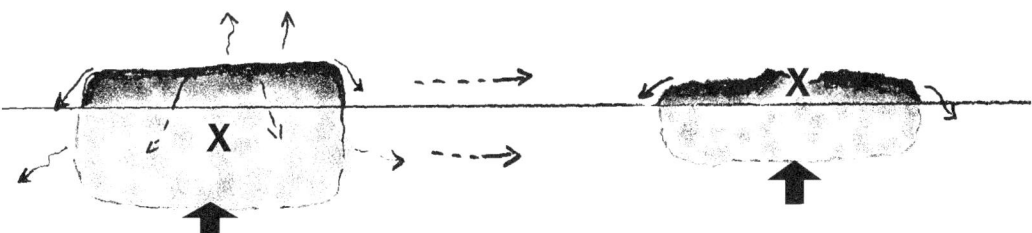

**Floating ice cubes** act like the continents floating on the Earth's mantle. As the ice melts, the cubes are buoyed higher up in the water. The position of the "X" changes from the middle of the cube to the surface. Erosion of the ancestral Grenville mountains allowed the deep root rocks to eventually get to the surface.

# 6   Why the Adirondacks Look the Way They Do

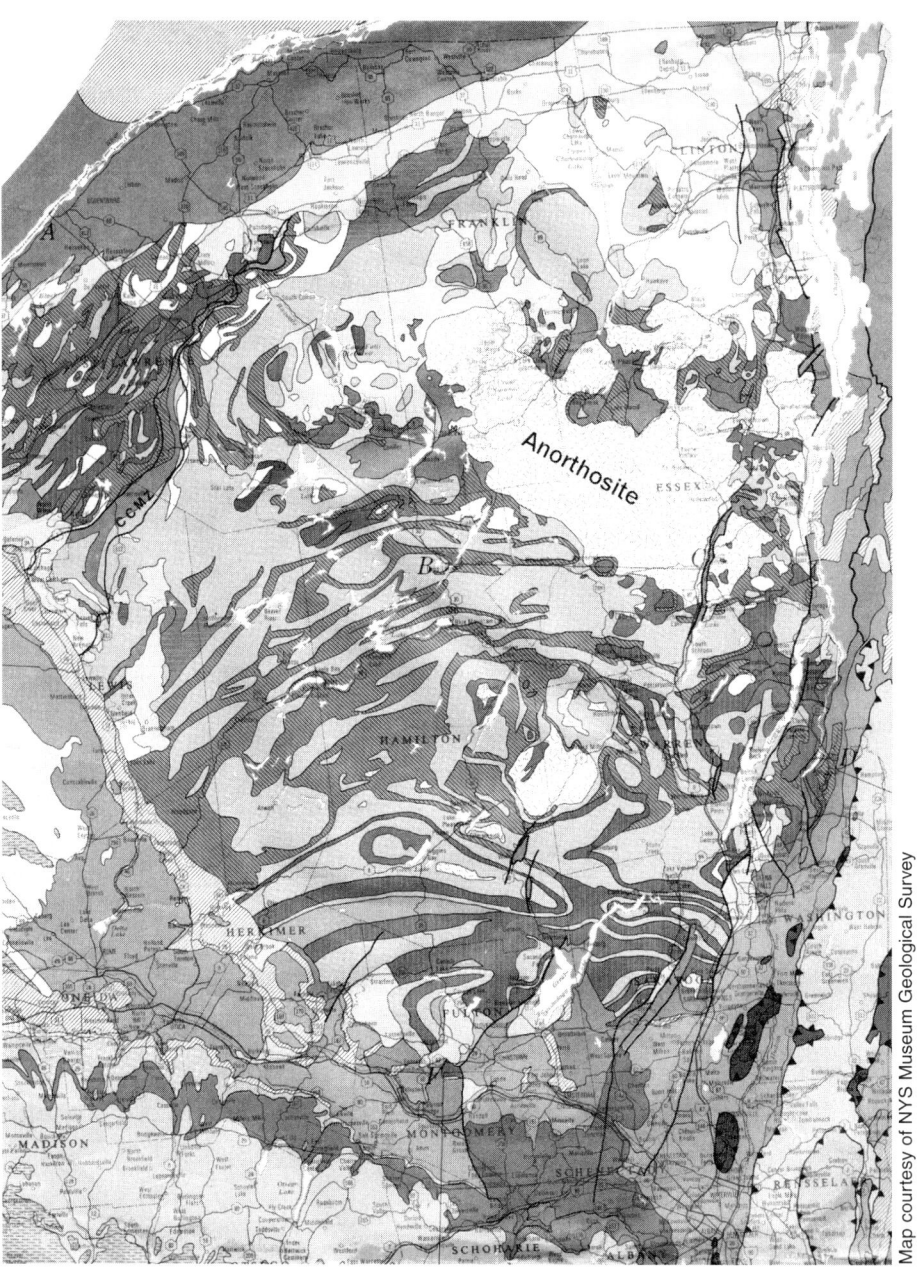

**The geology map of the Adirondacks** has the appearance of a slice of saltwater taffy, with giant swirls of various rock types intermixed. The magma intrusion of anorthosite is distinctive, as well as the much younger sedimentary rocks of the St. Lawrence Valley to the north.

years. Above, a towering mountain chain grew, extending from what is now Labrador to Texas. This mountain-building episode is called the Grenville Orogeny. Geologists see a close analogy where the sub-continent of India is colliding with Asia, uplifting the Himalayan Mountains and the Tibetan Plateau, a two-continent thickness of crust that launches the highest mountains in today's world.

The pressure-cooked rock was pulled, folded and squeezed like a giant batch of saltwater taffy, as evidenced in the geologic map of the region. Internal molten rock, or magma, also intruded into the semimolten sedimentary rock and added a swirled mix of different rock. All this rock was heated and then cooled together, metamorphosing into new rock. Limestone and dolostone (a sandy limestone) were changed to marble, shale to garnet and feldspar gneiss, and sandstone to quartzite. Magmas became tough metamorphic anorthosite, gabbro and granitic gneiss. The rock cooled and re-crystalized over several hundred million years. Overlying mountains were worn away, and deep-seated rocks were slowly buoyed toward the surface as the crust adjusted.

**Some Adirondack Rocks and Minerals**

Where very different rock types came in contact with each other and cooled, their boundary created unusual minerals. Wollastonite is a calcium silicate mineral created where limestones and silica-rich granites contact and crystalize together. This mineral is mined near Harrisville, in the northwest corner of the region, and near Lewis and Willsboro in the Champlain Valley. Wollastonite is a fibrous white mineral that is a safe asbestos substitute, used in ceramic, paper and paint manufacturing.

Iron ore, as the mineral magnetite, occurs in many places in the Park. This dense black mineral is very high grade iron ore and was mined at Star Lake, Lyon Mountain, Mineville and Witherbee, up to the late 1960s.

# Why the Adirondacks Look the Way They Do

## Adirondack Geology Time Line

- -1.6 million years ago to present. Ice-age glaciers cover the Adirondacks in four successive phases, gouging and molding the peaks and valleys into the present landscape.

- -10 million years ago. Hot spot develops in earth's crust below the Adirondack region; heated rock expands and uplifts the region in a giant dome. Overlying sedimentary rock erodes away, leaving ancient metamorphic rock at the surface, uplift estimated at over 7,000 feet total.

- -400 to 225 million years ago. Taconic and Acadian Orogenies uplift mountains to the east. Adirondack region remains below sea level and stable.

- -550 million years ago. Land sinks and is covered by shallow sea; hard bodied life evolves and is preserved in sandstone and limestone sediments that cover the entire Adirondack region.

- -600 million years ago. Continents separate and rifting causes massive faults and fracture lines in a north-northeast line up.

- Erosion strips away 50,000 ft. of mountain mass that reduces the region to near sea-level.

- 1.3-1.1 billion years ago. Continental collision uplifts original mountains and pressure-cooks the root zone now at the surface. Entire area is near the equator and tilted 90 degrees to the right.

## Modern Mountains from Ancient Rocks

**The abandoned titanium-magnetite mine at Tahawas** is a huge scar on the landscape just south of the High Peaks Wilderness. The Hudson River is meandering in the foreground.

## 10    Why the Adirondacks Look the Way They Do

**Magnetite sand grains** form the black lines along the water edge of many Adirondack beaches. The heavy magnetite sorts out by wave action, compared to the silica-feldspar grains that form the majority of beach sands.

At Tahawas, near the High Peaks, it combines with illmenite and was an important source of titanium during World War II. None of these mines is active today, and the iron industry that fueled the settlement of the Champlain Valley is a thing of the past. Magnetite grains form the distinctive black sand lines found on most Adirondack beaches. Magnetite is significantly heavier than silica sand and therefore settles out separately by wave action. You can pick up these black sand grains with a magnet.

Graphite was mined near Hague and Ticonderoga in the Lake George basin. This slick silver-gray mineral is pure carbon, like a diamond, but very soft because of its weak crystal lattice. Graphite is used as a lubricant and in steel manufacture, but it's best known as the "lead" in pencils. The Dixon-Ticonderoga Pencil Factory used graphite and cedar from the Champlain Valley to create its famous writing tools for more than a century. Research in the 1970s discovered that the abandoned iron and graphite mines are important hibernation sites for bats, and so New York State and the Nature Conservancy have been active in recent years in protecting the mines.

The intense metamorphism in the Adirondacks caused the mineral garnet to occur in many rock types. The Barton Mine at North River is the site of the most concentrated mass of garnets in a complex gneiss and gabbro rock. Although few of these garnets are of gem quality, when crushed the razor-edged crystals make one of the best abrasives known. If you purchase the red sandpaper made in the United States, it most surely is made of Adirondack garnet from the Barton Mine, just north of Gore Mountain. Polished black garnet-bearing gneiss slabs are also now marketed as exquisite kitchen counter and desk tops.

## 12   Why the Adirondacks Look the Way They Do

**The Old Barton Garnet Mine** near North River. The family business still gives tours during the summer months. Raw garnet crystals are easily observed here.

  Rocks are assemblies of minerals. The different chemical and crystal makeup of various minerals create the many rock types of the Adirondacks. Anorthosite is a tough igneous rock that weathers slowly and makes up most of the High Peaks area in the north Central part of the Park. There is a second exposure west of Indian Lake where Snowy Mountain is located. Made of more than 90 percent plagioclase feldspar, anorthosite is often composed of huge dark gray crystals set in a matrix of lighter fine crystals. Anorthosite is a relatively rare rock type on earth, but it is a most common rock on the face of our moon. Some anorthosite contains crystals of labradorite which are beautifully iridescent blue and yellow. The labradorite iridescence is caused by titanium atoms wedged in the plagioclase crystal lattice. Route 3 between Saranac Lake and Tupper Lake has been termed the "anorthosite highway" because most of the new rock cuts exhibit fresh faces of anorthosite. I've collected many

## Modern Mountains from Ancient Rocks 13

**Anorthosite road cut near the Ampersand Mountain Trailhead** parking lot on Route 3, about midway between Saranac Lake and Tupper Lake.

**Route 73 snakes** its way from Keene into Cascade Pass, gaining nearly 1,100 feet in elevation. Oak-covered Pitchoff Mountain Is on the right while the 4000-foot Cascade Mountain is on the left.

fine specimens of anorthosite and labradorite along this section of road. The falls area between the Upper and Lower Cascade Lakes on Rt. 73 is also known to produce exquisite labradorite crystals.

Marble is found in the central, northwestern and southeastern parts of the Park. Marble is made of calcium carbonate crystals (calcite) embedded with varying amounts of graphite and mica flakes. Some geologists believe that the graphite is a remnant of fossil blue-green algae that grew in the limey basin seas of the Grenville period, some 1.3 billion years ago. This white rock is easily dissolved in acidic water and weathers quickly, therefore it forms many of the valleys in the central part of the Park. Most of the bedrock exposed in the valley of Rich Lake at the Visitor Interpretive Center(VIC) at Newcomb is marble, and a fresh road cut can be seen about half-way between the VIC and the west edge of the ham-

**Like salt water taffy**, the narrow bands of gneiss and marble make the banded bedrock exposed distinctive along the Rich Lake shoreline at the Newcomb VIC.

## Modern Mountains from Ancient Rocks 15

**Potholes** etched in marble in the riverbed of the Trout River at Natural Stone Bridge and Caves at Pottersville.

**A good graphitic marble exposure** is in view east of the Newcomb Visitor Interpretive Center entrance on Rt. 28N before entering the hamlet of Newcomb.

### 16 Why the Adirondacks Look the Way They Do

let on Route 28N. Rich Lake supposedly got its name from the eroded grains of mica that shimmer like gold flakes on its beaches. A fascinating display of marble weathering and landscape formation is found at Natural Stone Bridge and Caves at Pottersville, where Trout Brook has eroded caves and crevasses among marble and gneiss folds.

Granitic gneiss is the most common rock in the Park and occurs in a variety of types and places. A metamorphosed granite, it is composed of quartz, feldspars, hornblende, biotite and other minerals and is extremely variable in appearance. Granitic gneiss is resistant to weathering and forms the ridges and mountains of the Park where it coincides with the valley-forming marbles. At the Newcomb VIC, many of the bedrock exposures of marble exhibit snakelike ridges several inches wide made of granitic gneiss. The late state geologist Yngvar Isachsen, who was an expert on Adirondack geology, once took me aside and said. "You know,

**Many knobby hills** of the eastern Adirondacks are classified as "exfoliation" domes, caused by granitic gneiss rock eroding away like the layers of an onion.

if a gneiss rock is heated too much, it becomes just another piece of schist!" I never forgot that message.

Complex metamorphic rock made from mixtures of Grenville sedimentary rock are also found throughout the Park. These calc-silicate gneisses are extremely variable, often strikingly beautiful and can exhibit fine specimens of quartz, calcite, phlogopite mica, pyrite, and other minerals. The stone quarry north of Saranac Lake on Rt. 3 is my favorite collection site in this rock type.

I urge anyone interested in rock-hounding and geology in general to get a copy of the New York State Museum's book The Geology of New York–A Simplified Account (educational leaflet number 28). This book and the accompanying geologic map are indispensable in learning the geology of the Adirondacks, and other places in New York. Yngvar Isachsen was one of the authors, and he was my friend and mentor when I was learning the geology here.

OK, let's pick up the story again and find out what happened to the rocks and minerals as time marched on. During the half-billion years of metamorphism in deep burial, the Grenville mountain mass above was worn away as it uplifted. Geologists calculate that mountains, on average, wear away at the rate of about one foot every thousand years. In the case of the Grenville mountains, the 50,000 feet of overlying rock was easily stripped down to the buried root zone.

At that time, some 600 million years ago, the region was a flat plain, worn down to sea level, with the beveled metamorphic root rock at the surface. The two sutured continents rifted, or split up, and an ocean basin began to flood the space between them. This rifting stretched and pulled apart the region's crust. Faults and fracture zones developed in the cool

## 18  Why the Adirondacks Look the Way They Do

**Avalanche Lake, wedged between Mount Colden and Algonquin Peak** lies in a steep narrow valley created in a fracture zone formed some 600 million years ago. The lake itself was created by the damming of glacial debris only about 11,000 years ago.

brittle rock that run in north to northeast trending lines that still persist today. Long Lake and Indian Lake are located in these straight fractured zones. Deep trenches of down-block faulted valleys, called grabens, hold spectacular lakes such as Lake George and Schroon Lake. Many of these fault lines can be traced on the landscape down into the eastern Finger Lakes, even though they are buried under thousands of feet of younger sedimentary rock. Because fracture zones erode easily, they often form the river and lake valleys of the Adirondacks.

As the continents separated, the Adirondack region sank and was covered by a shallow sea. This new continental shelf received sand sediment

## Modern Mountains from Ancient Rocks    19

**Indian Lake** (seen here from the south) lies in a long narrow straight fracture valley, as does similar Long Lake, which is a flooded portion of the Raquette River

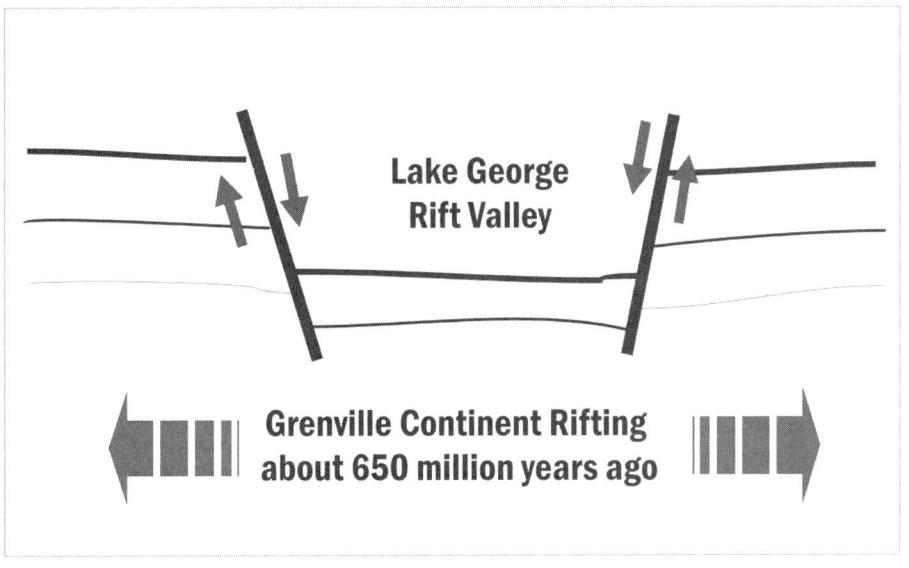

**Grabens**, such as the valleys of Lake George and Schroon Lake, were created by the stretching of the crust as this continent rifted some 650 million years ago. The vertical displacement at Lake George was nearly 1500 feet.

and eventually limey mud to a depth of several thousand feet. Hard-bodied organisms, such as trilobites, evolved at this time (the late Cambrian) and their fossils are common in the Potsdam sandstone on the north boundary of the Park. There are two fine examples of trilobite tracks in the sandstone floor of the VIC interpretive building at Paul Smiths. The sandstone was mined at Rainbow Quarry in Burke, NY, about forty miles north of the center, just outside the Adirondack Park. Sandstone of the same age is found inside the Park boundary at Ausable Chasm, where the post-glacial Ausable River has cut an impressive vertical-walled canyon during the last 10,000 years.

**AuSable Chasm** near Keeseville is a deep canyon cut in sandstone that creates vertical walls. The chasm, as we know it, is only about 13,000 years old.

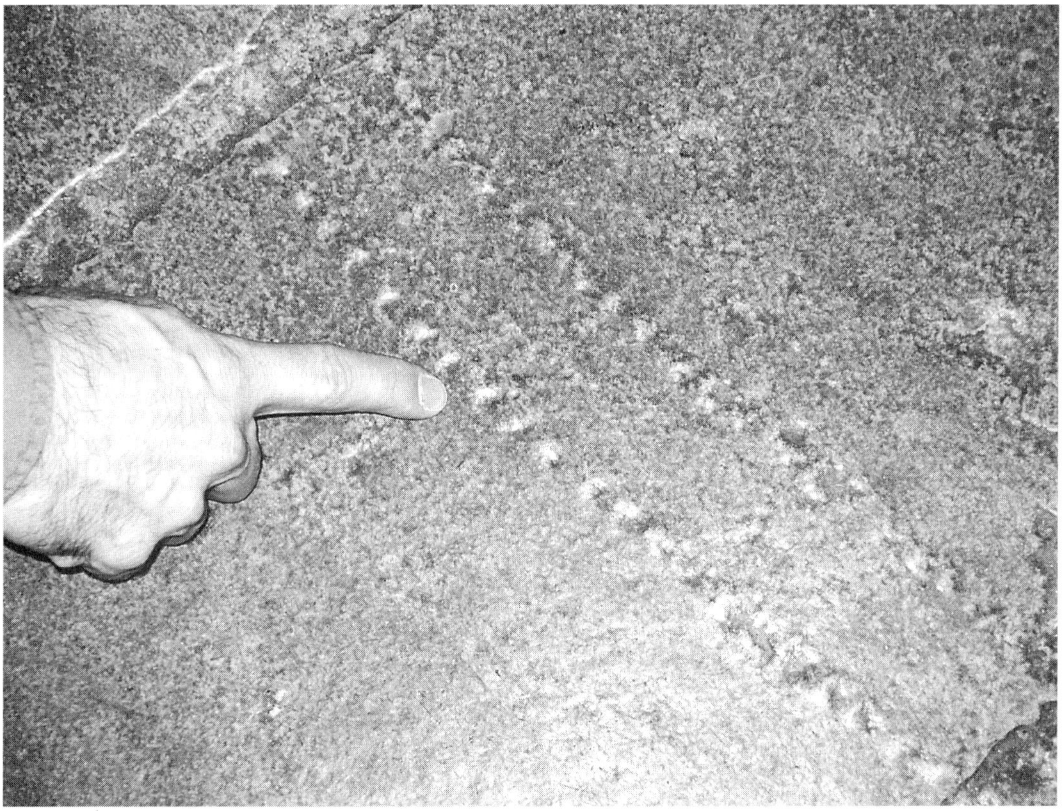

# Modern Mountains from Ancient Rocks    21

**Trilobite track** in the Potsdam sandstone that is used in the floor at the Visitor Interpretive Center at Paul Smiths.

**Trilobites** were the principal life form of the ocean bottom that covered the Adirondack region about 500 million years ago, when sandstones were deposited.

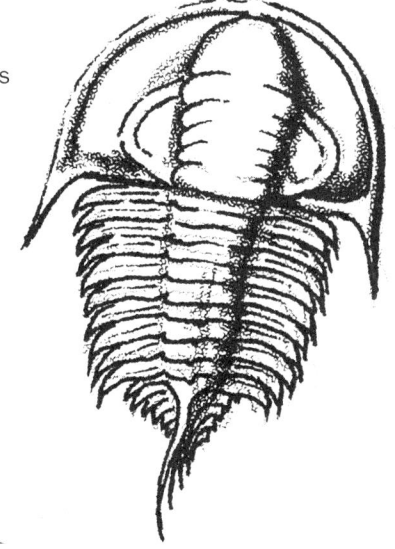

For a while, the Adirondack region became a geologically stable coastal plain. But other continental collisions occurred to the east and south. The Taconics, then the Green Mountains of Vermont and White Mountains of New Hampshire were uplifted. Eventually the whole Appalachian Range to the south was uplifted. The Adirondack region was too far inland to be affected by these episodes. There is no rock record of deposition or much erosion for the next 250 million years. To the east, the Atlantic Ocean was born as the continents rifted for the last time, about 180 million years ago. North America is still drifting away from Europe at a rate of one inch per year—nearly the same speed as your finger nails grow.

About ten million years ago, the Adirondack region began to be uplifted in a giant dome shape, about 120 miles long by 80 miles wide. Geologists now believe that a hot spot developed in the earth's crust deep below the Adirondack region, expanding the rock above it, and uplifting these new mountains at least 7000 feet. There is evidence for this theory from the carbonate springs at Saratoga, where the dissolved carbon dioxide in the water there is coming from deep in the crust, a situation that is found only in areas surrounding hot spots such as at Yellowstone and Hawaii. In the Adirondacks, the hot spot is still so deep that heat has not yet reached the surface. Only the expanded rock above it has manifested itself as a domed mountain mass, still rising at a rate of about three quarters of an inch per decade, faster than erosion is wearing it away. Using satellite imagery and other techniques, geologists have measured this rapid uplift during the past thirty years. Whether the uplift will continue or change in rate is anyone's guess.

This circular uplift is unique in North America. The major rivers flow out from the center like the spokes of a wheel. This pattern started early in the uplift sequence as the overlying flat sedimentary layers were eroded by running water. After several million years of erosion, those sand-

## Modern Mountains from Ancient Rocks    23

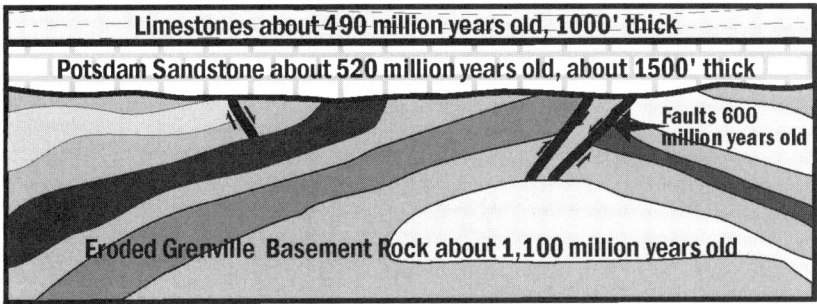

**Simplified cross-section of Adirondack Region about 15 million years ago.**

**Before the present uplift**, the Adirondack region was flat and at about sea level, covered with about 3000 ft. of sedimentary rock.

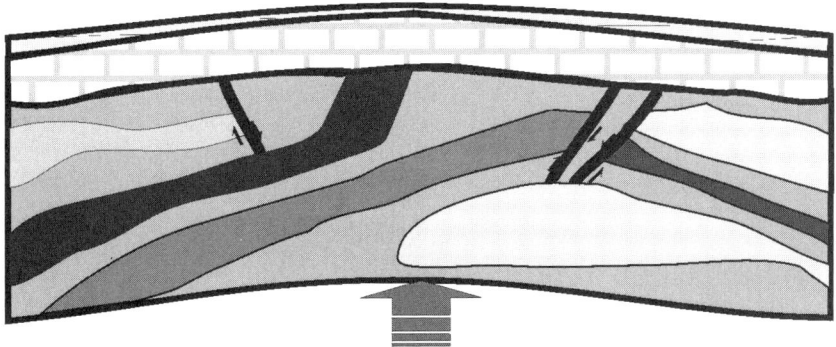

**Hot Spot Uplift beginning about 10 million years ago.**

**As the hot spot developed**, the region was uplifted above sea level and erosion began stripping the limestone and sandstone cover.

**Limestone exposure** west of Plattsburgh on Route 374. Here, you can see the tilted young sedimentary rock that once covered all of the Adirondack region until the current uplift began, only about 10 million years ago.

## 24  Why the Adirondacks Look the Way They Do

**Radial Drainage develops during early uplift in the 3,000 ft thickness of sedimentary rock lying over the Adirondacks about 10 million yrs ago.**

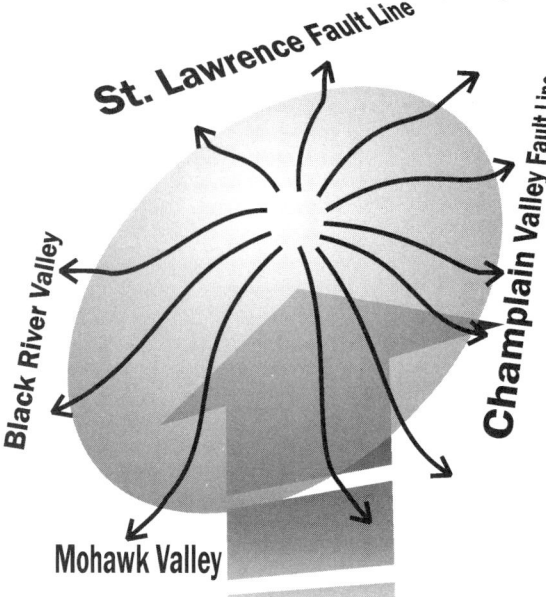

**The new dome** develops a radial drainage pattern, starting in the highest central area.

About 5 million years ago, erosion penetrated both the complex mix of rock types and the major and minor fault lines that crossed the Adirondack dome.

**As erosion continues**, rivers cut into the old metamorphic rocks, faults and fractures and bands of weak rock.

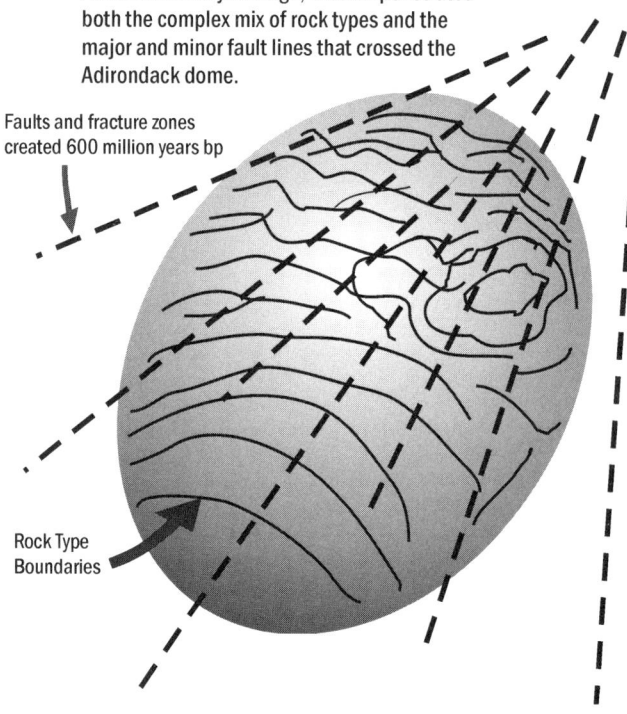

# Modern Mountains from Ancient Rocks

## Adirondack Uplift Sequence

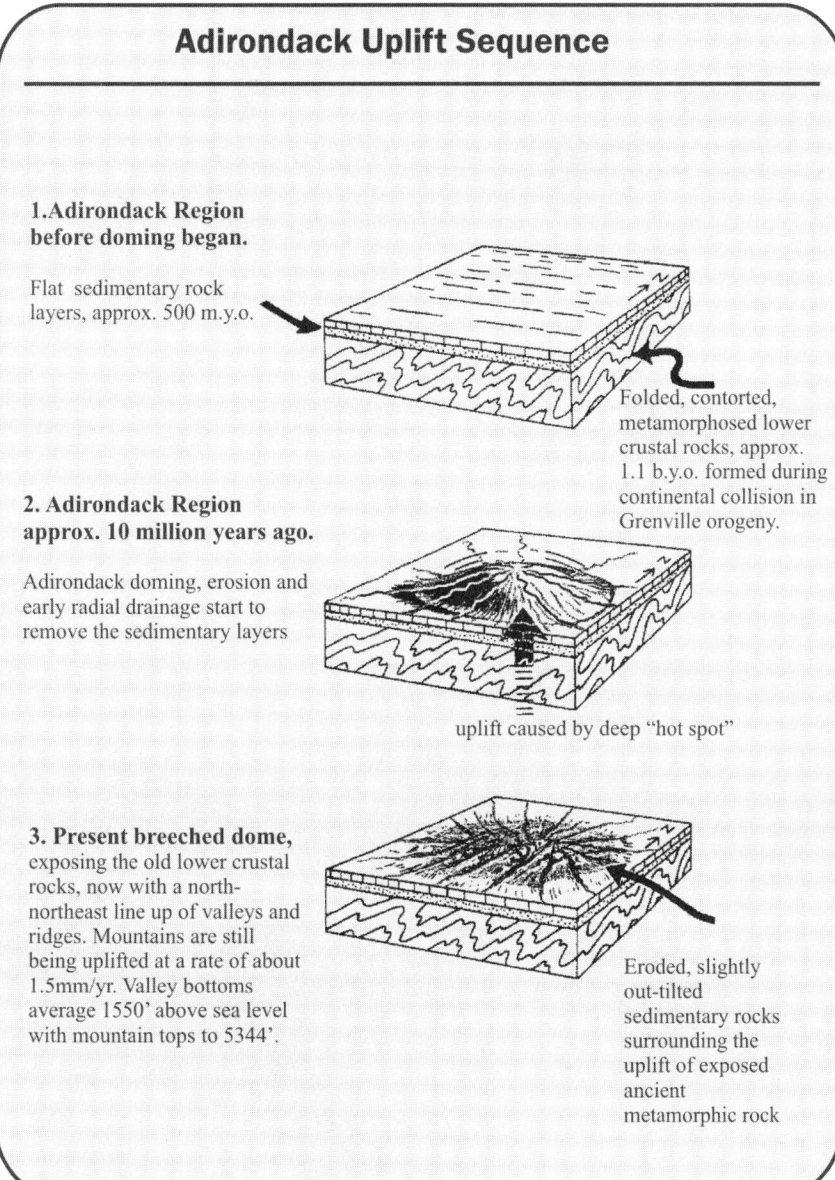

**1. Adirondack Region before doming began.**

Flat sedimentary rock layers, approx. 500 m.y.o.

Folded, contorted, metamorphosed lower crustal rocks, approx. 1.1 b.y.o. formed during continental collision in Grenville orogeny.

**2. Adirondack Region approx. 10 million years ago.**

Adirondack doming, erosion and early radial drainage start to remove the sedimentary layers

uplift caused by deep "hot spot"

**3. Present breeched dome,** exposing the old lower crustal rocks, now with a north-northeast line up of valleys and ridges. Mountains are still being uplifted at a rate of about 1.5mm/yr. Valley bottoms average 1550' above sea level with mountain tops to 5344'.

Eroded, slightly out-tilted sedimentary rocks surrounding the uplift of exposed ancient metamorphic rock

**Uplift sequence of the Adirondack Dome.** The process still continues today, with a yearly uplift of about 1.5mm.

## 26   Why the Adirondacks Look the Way They Do

**Blue Mountain Lake** is the beautiful headwaters of the Raquette River. The island-studded clear waters are a favorite for paddlers after a visit to the nearby Adirondack Museum.

**Lake Tear of the Clouds and Mount Marcy**. At an elevation of 4320 feet this boggy little pond is the highest permanent headwater of the mighty Hudson River.

**Today's drainage pattern** is still radial in look but modified by bedrock strength, fracture lines and, most of all, glacial damming that pushed rivers into new flow patterns about 11,000 years ago.

stone and limestone layers were stripped off, exposing the tough metamorphic rocks beneath. Now the rivers started eroding and following the fault lines formed during the rifting of the continent half a billion years earlier. The region now shows a radial drainage overprinted on a trellis pattern made up of major northeast fault lines and minor northwest breaks. Look carefully at a topo map of the Park and you'll see just how this works on rivers like the Boquet, Hudson and the Raquette. The rivers have not been working in this trellis pattern long enough to be totally controlled by strong and weak rock types, but given several more million years, that pattern will develop. Valleys occur where fault-fracture zones exist, and ridges tend to occur where the rock structure is competent.

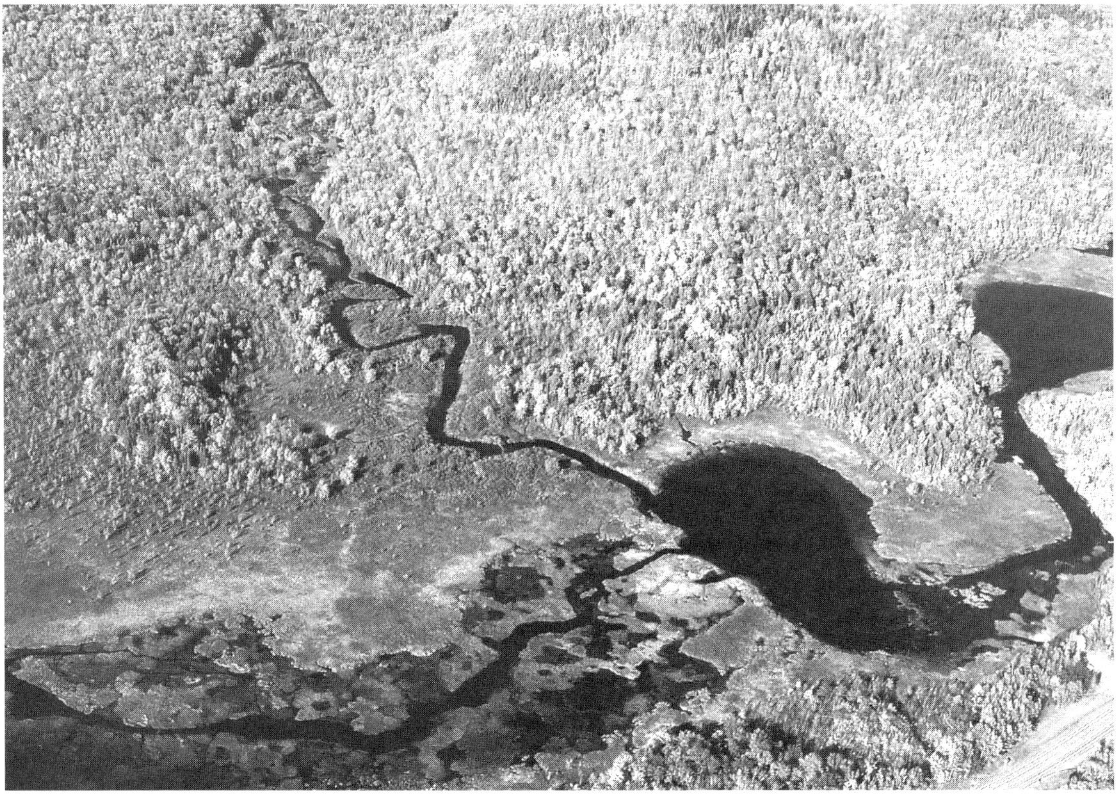

## 28   Why the Adirondacks Look the Way They Do

**The Kunjamuk River**, top left, enters a boggy kettle hole of the Sacandaga River, just east of Speculator on Route 30/8. Because of glacial features such as this, the drainage pattern of many rivers hold diverse habitats.

**The view from Crane Mountain** in the southeastern Adirondacks is always impressive and worth the steep but short climb to the top.

# Modern Mountains from Ancient Rocks    29

**Lampson's Falls** on the Grass River, (seen in a mid-summer flood) lies near the "fall-line" at the outer edge of the Adirondack uplift. Most big falls are found near the Park's edges—as geologic proof that the mountains are young, not yet eroded very far upstream.

Waterfalls are a product of headward erosion in a valley, with the stream or river cutting upstream faster than the valley widens as time passes. There tends to be many more waterfalls on the lower reaches of river valleys of the Adirondacks because so little time has passed in the uplift sequence. In fact, many are located just at the boundary of the Adirondack uplift, revealing the geologic youth of the mountains. But what about the interior falls that we see, like Raquette Falls north of Long Lake? Here, glacial damming forced the river to take a sharp left turn north of the lake and find a new route to the north and west, creating a waterfalls where one would not be expected. This glacial history will be explored in the next chapter, because it created so much of the familiar look of the Adirondack landscape.

## Living Geology...Earthquakes

In the three decades I've lived here, the Adirondacks have had two major earthquakes, each about 5 on the Richter scale. Both awoke my

**The Saranac River** (shown here near Redford) is one of the larger rivers of the Adirondacks. It holds two large hydropower generating impoundments between Saranac Lake and Plattsburgh.

**Modern Mountains from Ancient Rocks** 31

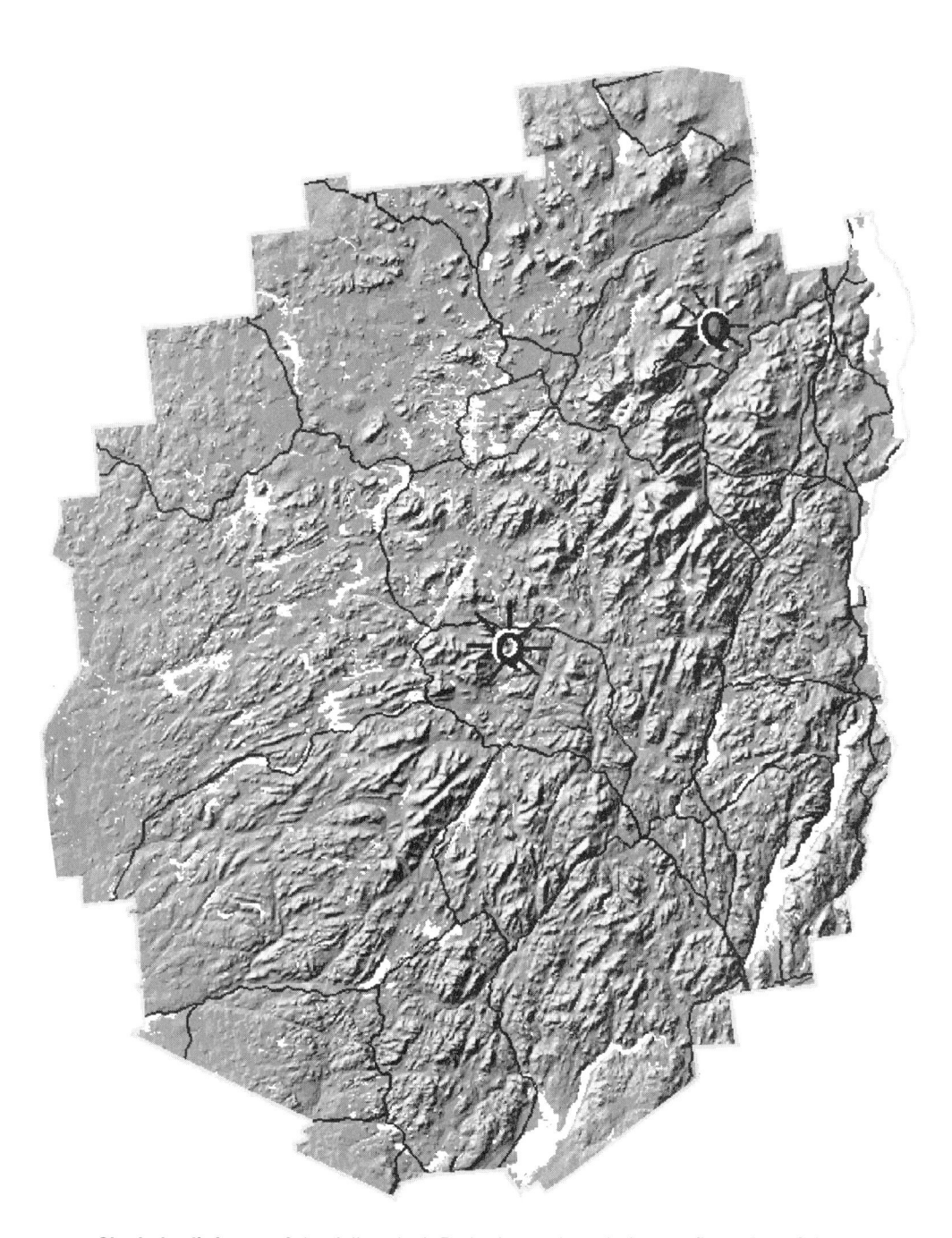

Shaded relief map of the Adirondack Park shows the relative configuration of the mountains, lakes, valleys and roads that we experience today. The two "Q's" locate the two large earthquakes of 1983 and 2002. Map courtesy the Adirondack Park Agency.

**Algonquin Peak** dominates this view from the Adirondack Loj Road outside of Lake Placid. Mount Colden is to the left; Indian Pass is to the right.

wife Joan and I at dawn. Each time, it sounded and felt as though a freight train were running through our house at 50 mph. Joan screamed, "What's happening?" as pictures crashed from the walls and the chairs shook in circles. I had experienced tremors when I was a ranger in Yellowstone, so I had an inkling of what was happening. The first occurred on October 7, 1983 with an epicenter several miles west of Newcomb. The second one was on April 20, 2002 with an epicenter about five miles north of Ausable Forks.

Adirondack earthquakes differ from Pacific Coast/California earthquakes in the depth of the quake and the bedrock in which they occur. Quakes here are shallow, about three to four miles down and in brittle, "cool" rock. California quakes are often 15 to 50 miles deep and in "warm" rock. Quakes here involve intense rapid vibration, with little deep rocking and rolling at ground level and seldom crack the surface to betray a fault line. The bedrock sends these vibrations great distances—both quakes were felt in New York City, more than two hundred miles away.

Earthquakes tell us that the Adirondack landscape is still alive, responding to the pressures of heat expansion of the bedrock. What this bodes for the future of the mountains over the next millennia is anyone's guess.

Thus, the Adirondacks are brand new mountains, still pushing up faster than they are wearing away, made of ancient one-billion year old rock. This combination of old rock and new mountains is not unusual. The Grand Teton Mountains in Wyoming are made of 2.5 billion year old rock, thrust up only in the last million years. Mount McKinley in Alaska is old rock in new mountains that are uplifting at about the same rate as here in the Adirondacks. The bedrock foundation was formed, and the sculpturing by water, wind and ice would continue to shape the Adirondack region to look different from every other place.

# Why the Adirondacks Look the Way They Do

## Chapter 2 The Age of Ice

The Pleistocene era, starting about 1.6 million years ago, gave rise to the glaciers that profoundly shaped today's Adirondacks. Evidence suggests that there were few or no lakes here because the rivers at that time had just cut through the overlying uniform sedimentary rock in a rather smooth and orderly fashion. Lakes don't appear on the landscape without a cause. Just look on a map of North America and you can see where natural lakes exist: almost entirely in places that where glaciated.

Residents here have little trouble accepting that the Adirondacks have been covered by thousands of feet of ice most of the past million and a

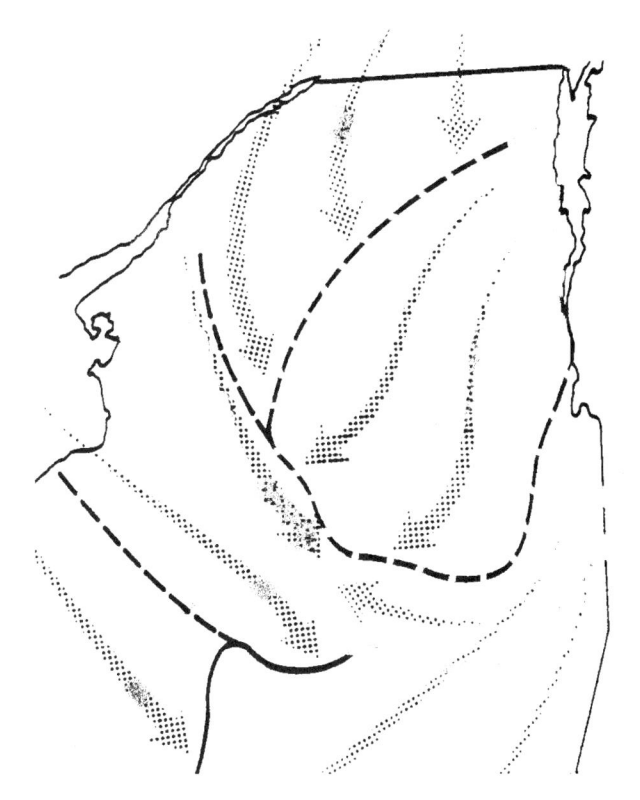

**Several ice sheet lobes** swept over the Adirondacks, and moving in different directions. Where the Champlain lobe and the St. Lawrence lobe met is where the Adirondack lake country exists today.

half years—every tough winter is a brief reminder of this glacial time! Each of the four successive continental ice sheets that formed over North America in the Pleistocene masked the changes wrought by the earlier ones, so we will only be concerned with the last "Wisconsin" glacial period. This swept over the Adirondacks between 40,000 and 11,000 years ago with ice nearly two miles thick.

The lobes of ice that covered the Adirondacks started to pile up southeast of Hudson's Bay and began to spread in all directions like a huge mass of pancake batter. In this region, the 10,000-foot-thick ice was funneled down the Champlain and St. Lawrence lowlands, eventually overriding the mountains and flowing in a southwesterly direction. The flow followed the northeast-trending fault and fracture zone valleys, greatly eroding these weak-rock areas. The bottom of Lake Champlain was gouged out to as much as 245 feet below sea level. Previous to glacial action, evidence at Lake George suggests that it was once two separate river systems whose divide was in the "narrows" east of Tongue Mountain, one river flowing north and the other south. Glacial erosion cut through that divide and connected the two systems into one watershed. Today, the lake is formed because of a glacial gravel dam south of Lake George, forcing all water to drain north through the La Chute River at Ticonderoga.

At its peak, about 22,000 years ago, the ice pushed all the way to northern Pennsylvania, New Jersey and Long Island. In New York State, only a small area in the southwest corner, now Allegheny State Park, was untouched by the ice sheet. The ice sheet end-moraine deposits to the south and east formed the gravel soils and sand beaches of Long Island, Cape Cod and Martha's Vineyard. Sea level was 350 feet below what it is today, since much of the earth's water was locked up in the continental ice sheets.

Glacial ice is not like a crystal-clear ice cube from your freezer compartment. The lower thousand feet of ice is chock-full of crushed rock,

## The Age of Ice 37

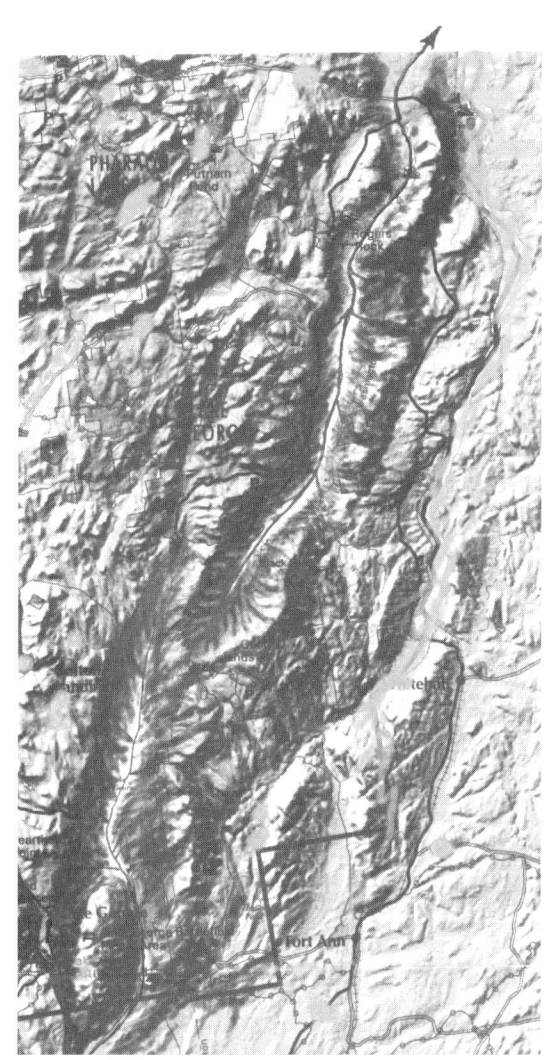

**Pre-glacial Lake George Region** held no lake, only two small river systems, with one flowing north and one flowing south.

**Ice erosion cut through the divide** between Tongue Mountain and Shelving Rock Mountain. Glacial damming of the Dunham's Bay outlet created Lake George by raising the water level that found its northerly outlet through the La Chute River at Ticonderoga.

**Glacial Ice 20,000 years ago**

Embedded sand and boulders

Bedrock

**Today's Landscape**

Mineral soil

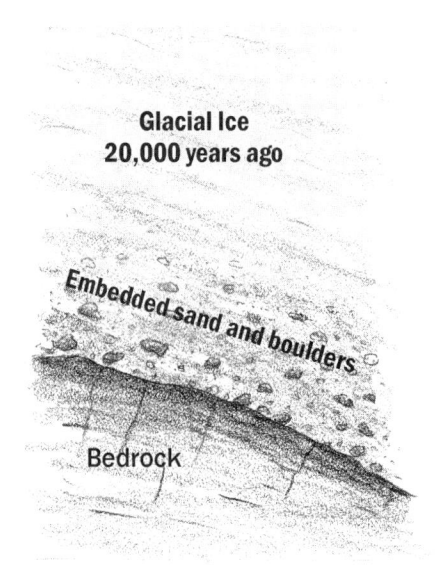

Bedrock

As glacial ice swept over the landscape it picked up chunks of rock and moved them to new locations to the south.

Once the ice melted, it left a sandy mineral soil and many large boulders known as glacial erratics.

sand, boulders, and clay. As a glacier moves, the zone of ice in contact with bedrock is in a constant re-crystalizing mode that grasps and plucks rock from the earth's surface and scrapes the bedrock like a giant sheet of sandpaper. Mountaintops were worn down, valleys were deepened, and surface rock was ground down and broken apart, with the pieces bulldozed miles to the south. The large boulders we see on the landscape are known as glacial erratics, a term that describes rocks that are not made of the same rock that makes up the local bedrock landscape.

During its advance, the ice rounded off the north sides of ridges and hills and plucked rock from the south-facing slopes, creating the many steep rock cliffs we see today. Apparently the High Peaks created a powerful obstruction that fragmented the advancing ice. An area near Tahawas was saved from strong ice scouring so that pre-glacial aged organic soils and tree wood more than 40,000 years old have been preserved there.

Starting about 19,000 years ago, the climate warmed and ended the

**Glacial Erratics**, the large boulders moved and left behind by the melting glacier, are scattered all over the Adirondack landscape in areas of till soil. They are often colonized by polypody ferns. Polypodys survive on the tops of erratics because the ferns are eaten by deer if they grow at ground level.

## Why the Adirondacks Look the Way They Do

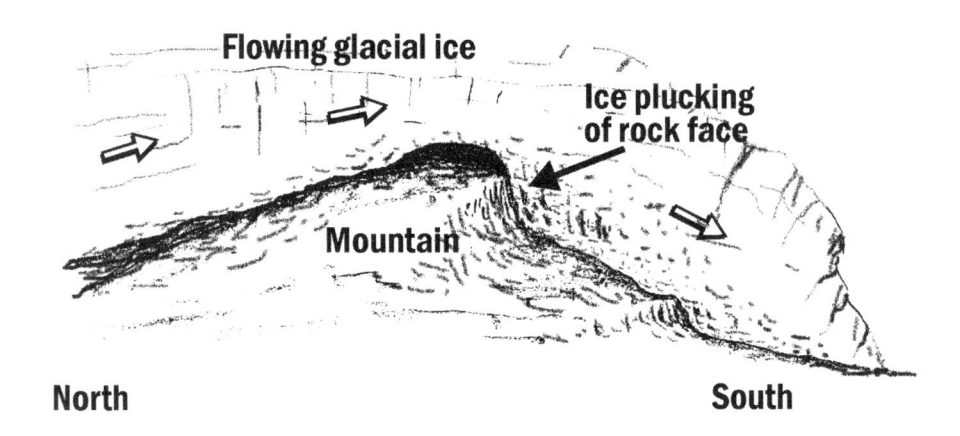

**As the ice moved south and overtopped the mountains**, the recrystalization of ice at the base tended to smooth the north sides of mountains and pluck rock from the south faces, creating the many steep open cliffs common on south-facing slopes.

**Silver Lake Mountain**, in the north-central Adirondacks, exhibits open cliffs created when glacial ice plucked rock away from the south-facing slopes. The lower cliff in this picture was a historic eyrie of peregrine falcons and was used in the early 1980s for reintroducing falcons to the region.

advance of the ice sheet. The long retreat of glacial ice began, a process that would take nearly 10,000 years to melt out of New York State and the Adirondacks. In the Finger Lakes, Hudson Valley, and Champlain Valley, the ice melted back in successive stages that caused massive debris piles (moraines) to be created. These moraines dammed the valleys at certain places. In the Finger Lakes, moraines developed at what are now the head and foot of each lake, damming the drainage and creating the beautiful Finger Lakes wine country of New York. Glacial Lake Albany covered the Hudson Valley from north of New York City to Glens Falls in a deep freshwater lake that lasted nearly 5,000 years.

The jumble of Adirondack mountains caused the ice to stagnate and melt from the top down, rather than retreat in linear stages as in other parts of the state. Linear moraines are nearly non-existent here, but the debris left by the stagnant glacier created the lake-dotted country we know and admire today. Remember that the bottom thousand feet of ice was packed with sand, clay, boulders, and rock fragments that were dropped or washed out of the melting ice. Let's take a look at some of these glacial features which can still be seen everywhere on the Adirondack landscape.

Glacial features are especially common in what I call the Adirondack Lake Country. If you draw a line from Old Forge to Lake Placid, the land northwest of this diagonal holds most of the classic canoe waters for which the Adirondacks are justly celebrated. The Lake Country is there because of the way the ice retreated. As the ice melted (top down), the High Peaks and the line of other major mountains such as Blue Mountain, Blue Ridge, Snowy and others blocked the flow of ice and meltwater. Water backed up between the mountains and the ice edge to the north, causing ephemeral glacial lakes to form, some deep and some shallow.

A deep glacial lake filled Keene Valley, whose outlet was south, through the Ausable Lakes valley, but dammed by debris to the south and by ice at the Wilmington area. If you drive Route 73 from Lake

# 42    Why the Adirondacks Look the Way They Do

**Wire rock-filled baskets**, known as gabions, mark the location of glacial lake delta deposits below Cascade Pass on Rt 73.

Placid to Keene, through Cascade Pass, you'll pass through several gravel and sand deposits. These are located by the wire rock-filled baskets (gabions) that retain the sand in the road cuts.

Another higher-level glacial lake existed just east of the village of Lake Placid. The flat field where the horse show grounds are located, and where the 1980 Winter Games opening ceremonies took place, was once the bottom of a glacial lake whose outlet was south through Indian Pass. The ski jumps at Intervale are built on gravel delta deposits that mark the high water level of that vanished lake. Hundreds of small and large glacial lakes must have dappled the landscape as the ice wasted away during the two thousand years it took to deglaciate the Adirondacks.

**John Brown's Farm, and the nearby Olympic ski jumps**, are located on a gravelly delta bench that extended into the high-level glacial lake that covered the eastern Lake Placid region.

## 44  Why the Adirondacks Look the Way They Do

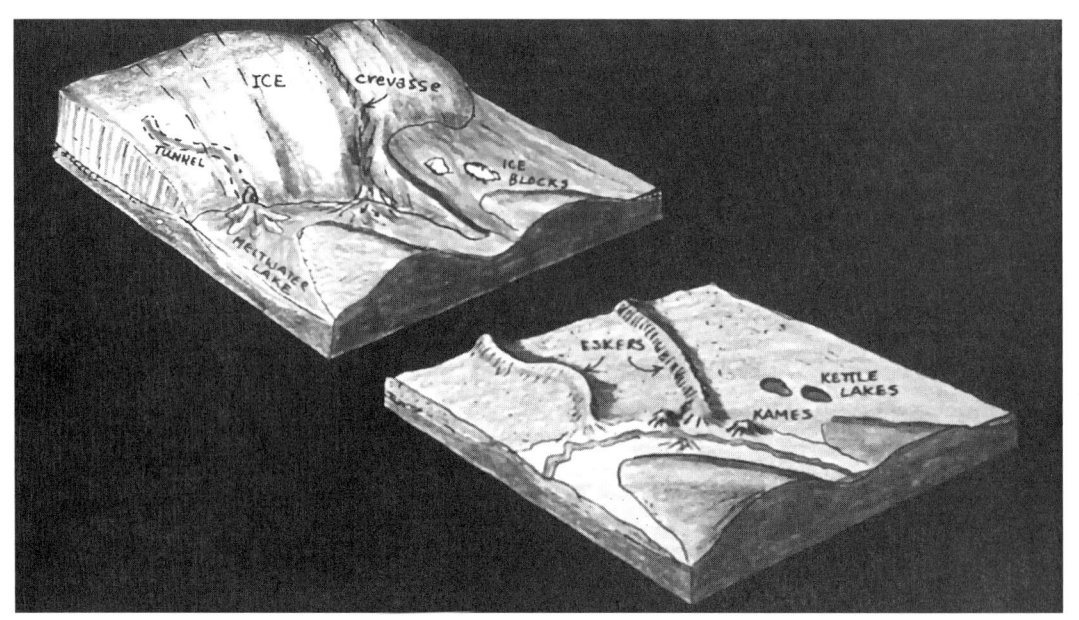

**As the ice sheets thinned and melted away**, various features were formed that can still be clearly seen on the Adirondack landscape.

Many glacial features seen today were formed as the ice thinned to less than 500 feet thick. Meltwater poured from the wasting ice and was saturated with rock debris, from tiny pebbles to cobbles the size of bowling balls. Where the flowing water was squeezed through a crevasse or tunnel in the ice, an esker resulted. An esker is a snakelike ridge deposit of a vanished glacial riverbed. They can be just a few feet high, but are often as much as 100 feet tall and many miles long. Eskers are found throughout the Park, but they are most common in the rolling lake coun-

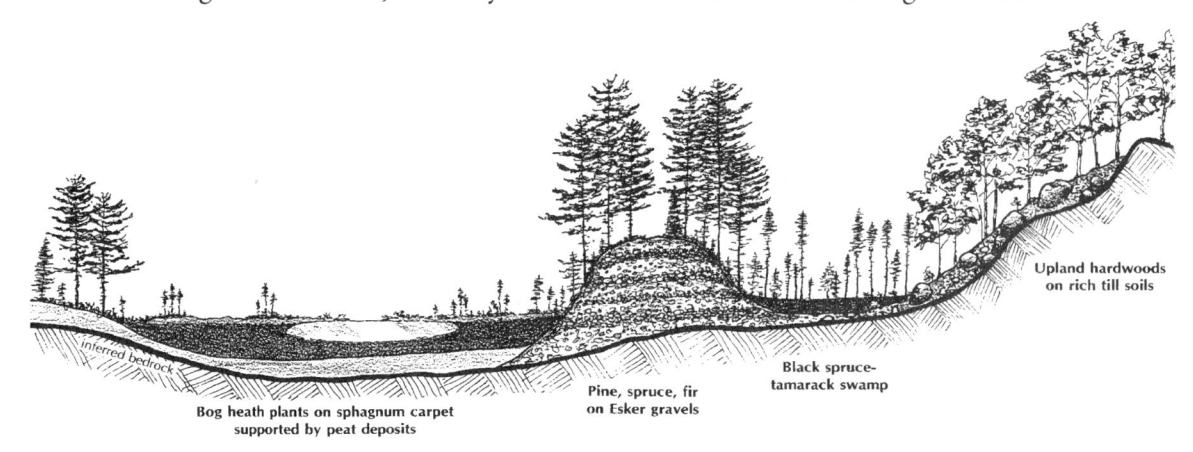

**Many glacial features** are often assembled together, since the process of formation can create conditions for kettle lakes, eskers, and bogs all at once, depending on the melting sequence of the ice, and the bedrock landscape that it covers.

## The Age of Ice 45

**Rainbow Lake Esker** splits Rainbow Lake from Clear Pond. The sandy ridge is clothed in red pine and other trees. The waterbodies on either side are considered kettle lakes, formed by ice bands adjacent to the meltwater esker river.

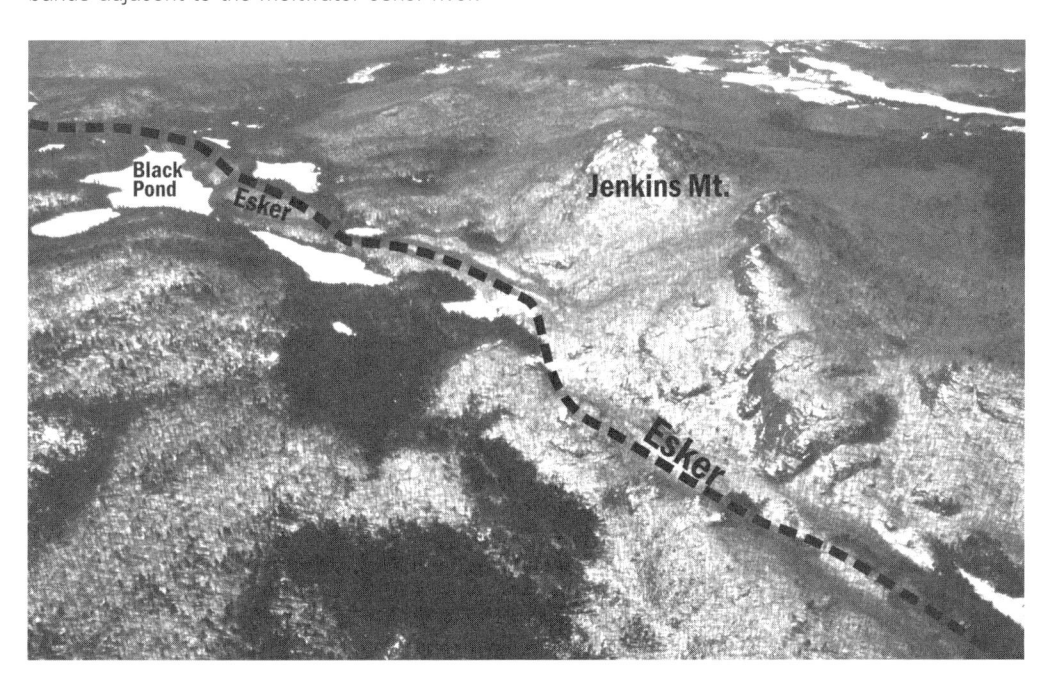

**Jenkins Mountain Esker** lies at the base of the mountain. This esker is made of two or three parallel ridges which join to form the single ridge next to Long and Black ponds in the upper far left. There are hiking, snowshoe and ski trails on this esker, located at the Visitor Interpretive Center at Paul Smiths.

**Half-filled in early autumn**, this kettle hole completely fills in Spring, then slowly empties as groundwater levels drop during summer. There is no inlet or outlet in this kettle located at the Paul Smiths VIC.

try of the central and west regions. The term esker is an Irish word for pathway—eskers were the dry ground paths on which peat miners used to travel across the Irish landscape. There, as here, glacial eskers course across the soggy landscape, crossing bogs, splitting lakes and tracing for miles the route of a long-vanished river. Some noteworthy eskers are at Five Ponds, Rainbow Lake, Massawepie, the Paul Smiths VIC and the ridge upon which great Camp Topridge is built.

Other glacial features are associated with eskers because they are often formed during this melting process. Kettle holes were formed when isolated chunks of ice (bergs) were buried in gravel and sand deposits. When

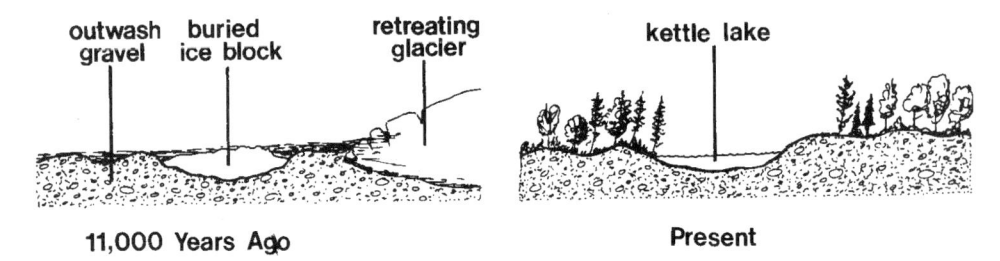

**Kettle lake formation**

**Kettle lakes** are formed when an iceberg is stranded and covered with outwash, then later melts, leaving a depression that sometimes fills with water. Kettles may be only a few feet wide, or many hundreds of feet in width and several miles long.

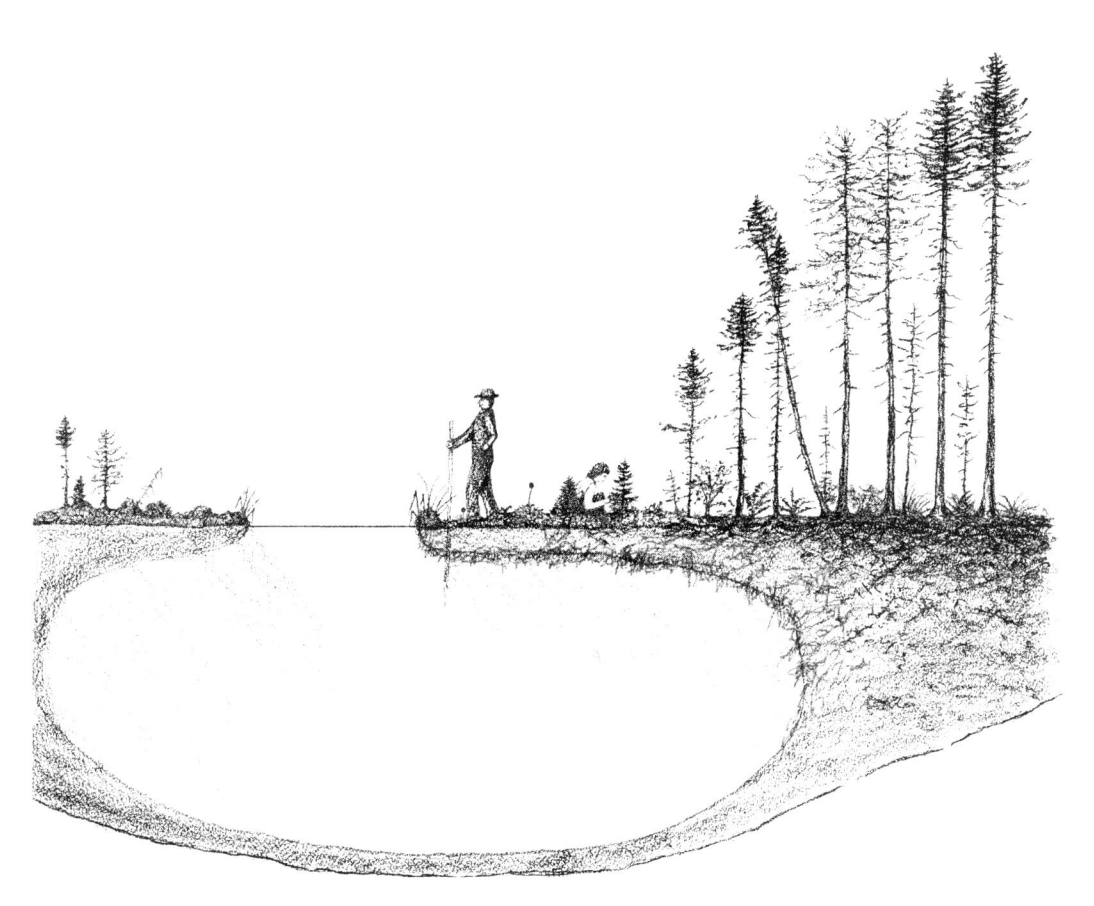

**Bog cross-section** shows growth of bog mat over the water. Accumulation of peat closer to shore is already thick enough to support the growth of larger trees. Given enough time, trees will completely cover the peat-filled depression.

the chunks melted, the resulting depressions filled with water if they were below the water table, with no direct surface inlet or outlet. Stagnant bog ponds were created in this fashion. If the depression is in a drainage system, a pond is formed and connected to other bodies of water. Some places have numerous connected ponds and small lakes in close proximity—the St. Regis Canoe Area is a prime example of what geologists call pitted outwash plains. These areas of sandy outwash deposits dotted with glistening water make many Adirondack canoe trips so enjoyable—good fishing, good swimming, great camping.

**The Saint Regis Canoe Area** is a kettle lake complex of kettle ponds in a massive outwash deposit south and west of Paul Smiths.

Spring Pond Bog and Massawepie Mire are huge depressions that were ice-choked meltwater lakes. The Gale Cemetery on Route 3, just north of Massawepie, is located on a glacial lake delta that indicates the height of water in what is now a vanished lake. The esker at Massawepie is one of the best examples of a classic Adirondack glacial feature that I've seen, and one that you can drive atop on a curvy dirt road in spring and fall. The steep slopes that drop off next to the road there are memorable.

Many Adirondack lakes and beaches owe their existence to eskers and related sand-gravel deposits. Long Lake is dammed at the north end by a truncated deposit across the Raquette River, just before connecting with the Cold River. The beautiful wild Middle Saranac Beach is built of wave-transported sand from an eroded esker at the east end. The Tioga Point beach on Raquette Lake, that creates Eldon Lake, was also built from a truncated esker. There are countless others scattered through the lake

**The Canoe Area ponds** are connected by small streams or short carries, making this wild area popular with paddlers seeking solitude and quiet times.

## 50  Why the Adirondacks Look the Way They Do

**Massawepie Esker** is a huge deposit that has a road built on top. Viewing the steep slopes down to the ponds is a memorable experience. The large bog complex in the distance is Massaweepie Mire, the headwaters of the Grass River.

**Gale Cemetery** about a half-mile east of the Massawepie Scout Camp entrance is located on a glacial sand deposit that marks the high-water level of the glacial lake that filled the basin during esker/kettle lake formation.

country—perhaps you also know some special places like these. The Park's 2,900 lakes and ponds glittering in the forest are vivid testimony to the powerful sculpturing wrought by the glacier.

As the retreating ice sheet thinned, the glacier occupied only the valleys and covered the lower hills of the Adirondacks. The higher peaks stood as islands in a sea of ice and meltwater lakes. Although the climate

**Middle Saranac Lake** and the upper Saranac River. The wild Middle Saranac Lake Beach is located just above the small esker that juts into the lake in the upper right side of the photo. Sand for the beach was transported by wave action from the eroded esker. You can paddle to the beach or hike the half-mile trail from the Ampersand Mountain Trail parking lot.

by this time (12,000 years ago) was similar to today's, more snow fell on the exposed mountaintops and small alpine glaciers formed and persisted for perhaps a thousand years. Each small glacier carved out a hollow and created a near-vertical headwall.

On Whiteface Mountain, for instance, there are three steep-walled hollows which geologists call cirques. Whiteface gets its name from an 1830 landslide that exposed the white anorthosite rock in the headwall of the south-facing cirque. If you drive up the Veterans Memorial Highway

**The summit of Whiteface** is marked by three bowl-shaped cirques, the result of small mountain glaciers that formed on the summit for about a thousand years following the melting of the main ice sheet. Cirques create steep headwalls that are subject to landslides and snowslides, which is how Whiteface got its name.

**The Summit of Giant Mountain** exhibits the many open shear slopes of glacial cirques.

to the upper lot and take the trail to the top, you'll be scaling the narrow spine (arete) between two cirques. If these alpine glaciers had persisted for several thousand years, the profile of Whiteface would have been sculpted similar to the Matterhorn in the Swiss Alps. Many other high Adirondack mountains have cirques (and slides) exposing their usually hidden bedrock.

At the height of glaciation, when the continental ice sheet was at least 10,000 feet thick covering the land, the earth's crust sank under the extra weight. In the St. Lawrence Valley, the land was depressed nearly 500 feet. Once the ice began to melt and thin out, the land gradually rebounded to its original elevation. (Picture your hand pressed on a down pillow, then lifted, to allow the pillow to fluff back to its earlier form.) This isostatic rebound of the crust was not uniform. There was less rebound to the south because the ice was thinner there. Geologists believe that the rebound occurred over a period of about 1500 years, ending some 10,000 years ago.

This timing was critical in the Champlain Valley, where the ice was backing northward. The land to the south was rebounding and a glacial lake formed, hemmed in by land near Whitehall and by ice to the north. The crust in the St. Lawrence Valley was still depressed below sea level. Much of the ice sheet had melted by 11,000 years ago, with ocean levels approaching their original depth. As the ice backed north, sea water then flooded into the Champlain Valley and converted the glacial lake to a salt water arm of the sea, as well as flooding the St. Lawrence Valley as far as Ogdensburg. Whales, sharks and seals swam in this arm of the sea for nearly 1,000 years. (Maybe that's when "Champ", the legendary monster of Lake Champlain, got into the lake.)

We can still find old marine beaches near Plattsburgh (now 350 feet above sea level) that contain shark teeth amongst the cobbles and stones. Eventually the crust in the Champlain Valley rebounded above sea level, and the lake converted back to the freshwater system of today.

So, the glacial epoch brought to this region the two dominant shapers of the landscape we see today. First, of course, was the ice itself. Second,

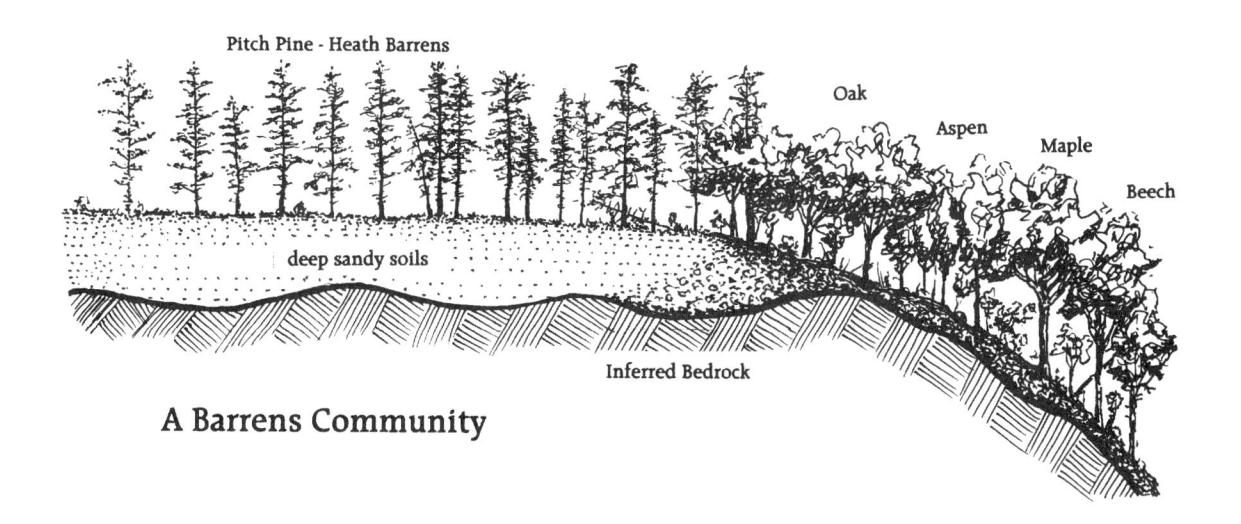

### A Barrens Community

**In the middle Champlain Valley,** pine barrens communities are found where sterile sand delta deposits perch on the upper edges of steep valleys. The sand was deposited when large glacial lakes successively occupied the Champlain Valley as the ice sheet retreated to the north. You can visit the Nature Conservancy's Clintonville Pine Barrens Preserve just east of Ausable Forks.

modern humans entered North America via the exposed land bridge that connected Alaska and Siberia some 25,000 years ago during the zenith of worldwide glaciation when sea levels were greatly lowered. The aboriginal Americans would inhabit nearly every corner of the continent long before the ice finally disappeared from Adirondack peaks.

**Soils—the connection of rock to life**

To most of us, soil is just dirt. But it is far more than just the stuff that gets tracked into the house in Vibram-soled boots. Soils are the vital link between geology and biology and govern the quality and quantity of life on any given piece of land. Adirondack soils are young, having developed only since the glacial retreat less than 12,000 years ago. Unglaciated areas in the rest of the United States south of New York have soils that developed over millions of years.

Soils are a combination of four basic ingredients: first, rock particles varying in size from clay particles to coarse sand and larger stones form the physical and chemical base. Organic matter, made of dead plants, animals and their wastes, form the second ingredient. The billions of living soil organisms, both large and small, make up the third part; and space for air and water is the last constituent.

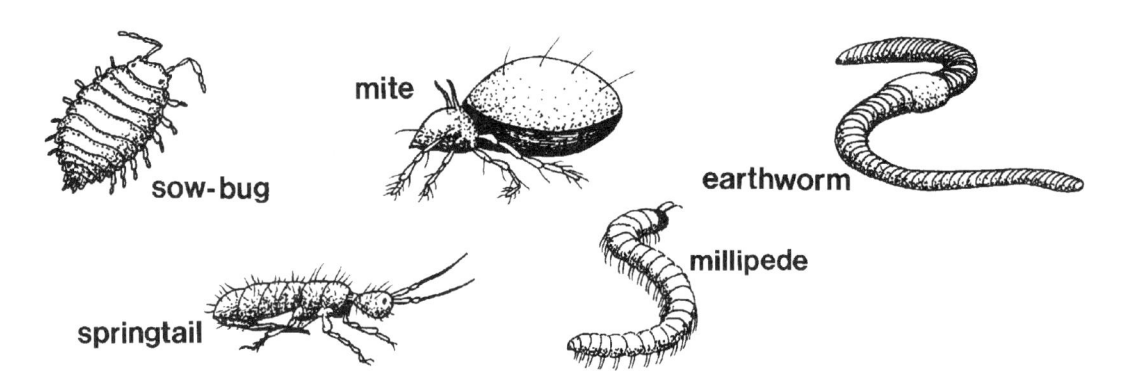

**Hidden life of the soil.** These organisms, and many others, act as the recyclers of the life above ground and are vital to the heath of the living soil.

Most of us think of soil only in terms of the first ingredient, the rock particles. But the living constituents of the soil keep it healthy and continually revitalize its life-giving properties. The recycling of nutrients in the top few inches of soil by soil organisms, such as bacteria, fungi, soil invertebrates and worms, sustains all the life more evident above the leaf litter. In February and March, skiers often encounter millions of snow fleas surfacing on sunny warm thaw days. This is usually the only time these tiny primitive soil insects are ever seen, for they remain hidden in the moist forest floor the rest of their lives, feeding on leaf litter and bacteria.

Each fall, for more than a decade, I taught a "recycling" lesson at the Paul Smiths VIC called the "Unnatural Trail" where we hid 25 human-created objects and had the students search for them along a forested path. After the search sequence, I'd ask them how long certain objects such as glass jars, plastic foam or paper might last in the woods before breaking down. I'd then have them pick up half-rotted leaves from the ground and ask, "How long ago did these fall and how old are they?" Most kids had never thought about those questions before. The age?..."Well, maybe a year." "No," I'd say; "When do leaves come out on the trees?" "Spring" "OK, when in spring?" "I think April." "No, later." We would finally agree that in the central Adirondacks, Memorial Day usually was the time of full leaf-out. So hardwood leaves are only about four months old when the tree discards them. "How long do leaves last on the ground once they fall in September?" "Five years..."ten"..."two." "Wrong." We'd talk about the speed at which organisms break down leaves and finally agree that most leaves become unrecognizable in less than a year. The cycle of life-death-life goes on constantly and quietly. But enough digression.

In the Adirondacks, soils are generally thin, acid and low in nutrients. This is due to the size and mineral makeup of the parent rock particles deposited by the glacier. Two major kinds of soils are present here: till and outwash. As the name implies, outwash soil is composed of particles

## Why the Adirondacks Look the Way They Do

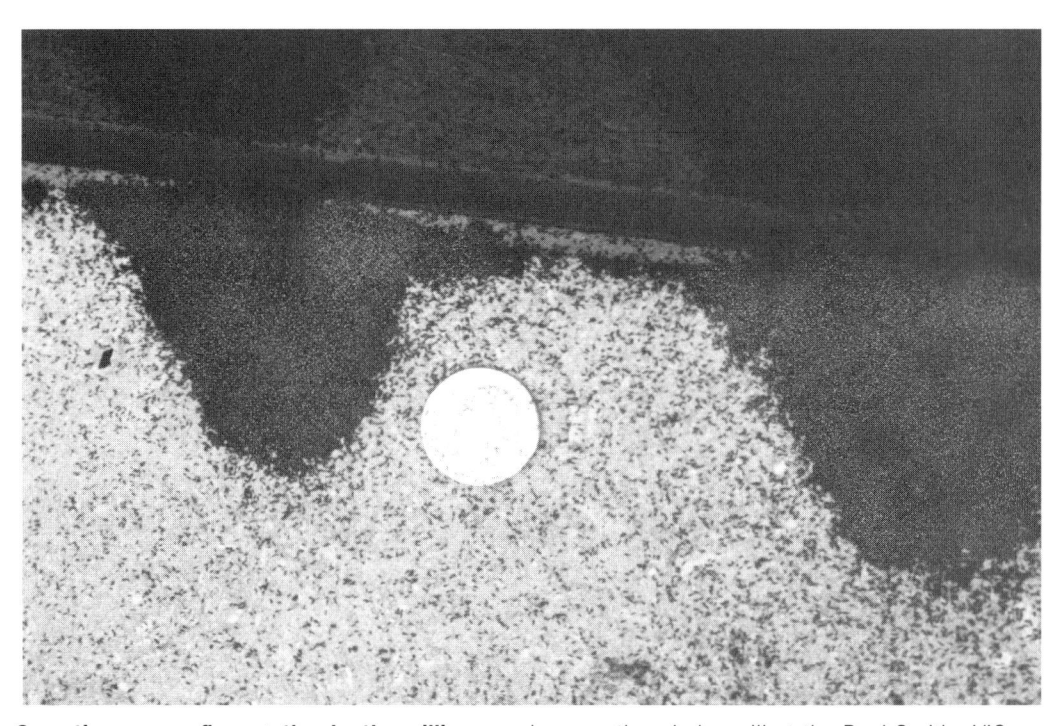

**Springtails** are tiny pepper-grain size soil insects that normally remain hidden, but on warm late winter days, they come to the snow surface and hop around using their abdominal "spring", hence the name snow flea.

**Sometimes snow fleas gather by the millions**, as here on the window sill at the Paul Smiths VIC. Each "wave" holds many thousands of snow fleas—compare to the quarter's size.

**Sand and gravel deposits** choke most valley floors in the Adirondacks and are commonly seen along the interior roads. Fine silt and clay particles were washed away in the torrents of water from the melting glacier, leaving the low-nutrient sand and gravels behind.

transported and deposited by running water coming from the melting ice. In the central Adirondacks, most valley bottoms range in elevation from 1,300 to 1,700 feet above sea level, and most are filled with outwash sand and gravel deposits. That's why there are so many gravel pits along the roadsides, since most roads in the Park are built in the valleys. Outwash soil is composed of large-sized sand and gravel. (The fine silt and clay particles, being held in suspension even in slow-moving streams, got carried away to the St. Lawrence and Champlain Valleys, and eventually, perhaps, to the Atlantic Ocean.) Outwash is very low-nutrient soil and subject to drought, so only evergreen trees and low-demand hardwoods can grow on it. Most of the glacial features described in the previous pages are composed of outwash.

## Why the Adirondacks Look the Way They Do

### Typical Soil Profile

**Outwash**
under evergreens

- litter layer
- humus
- leached layer
- deposition of leached material (often cemented, iron)
- oxidation

**Till**
under hardwoods

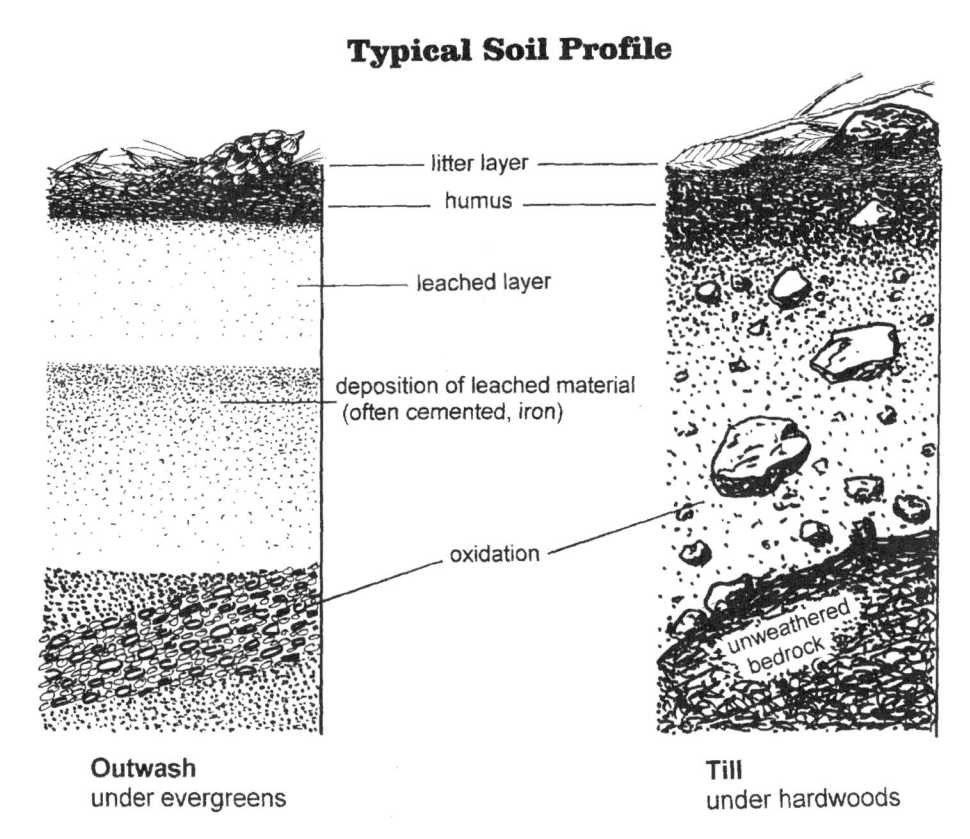

- unweathered bedrock

**Soil Profile** comparing outwash and till soil.

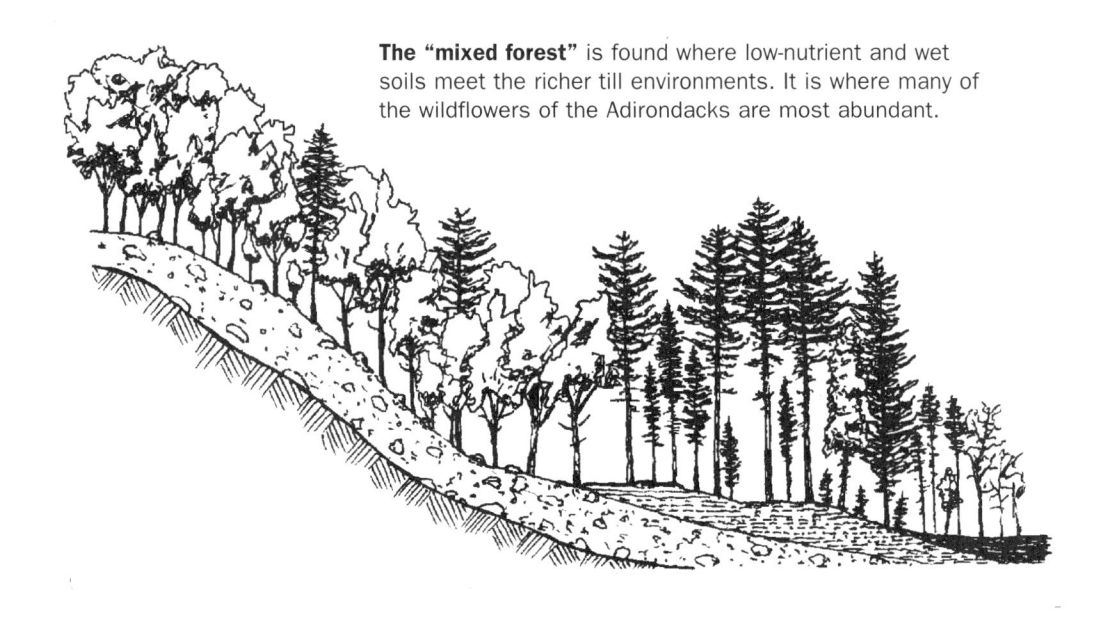

**The "mixed forest"** is found where low-nutrient and wet soils meet the richer till environments. It is where many of the wildflowers of the Adirondacks are most abundant.

The Age of Ice    59

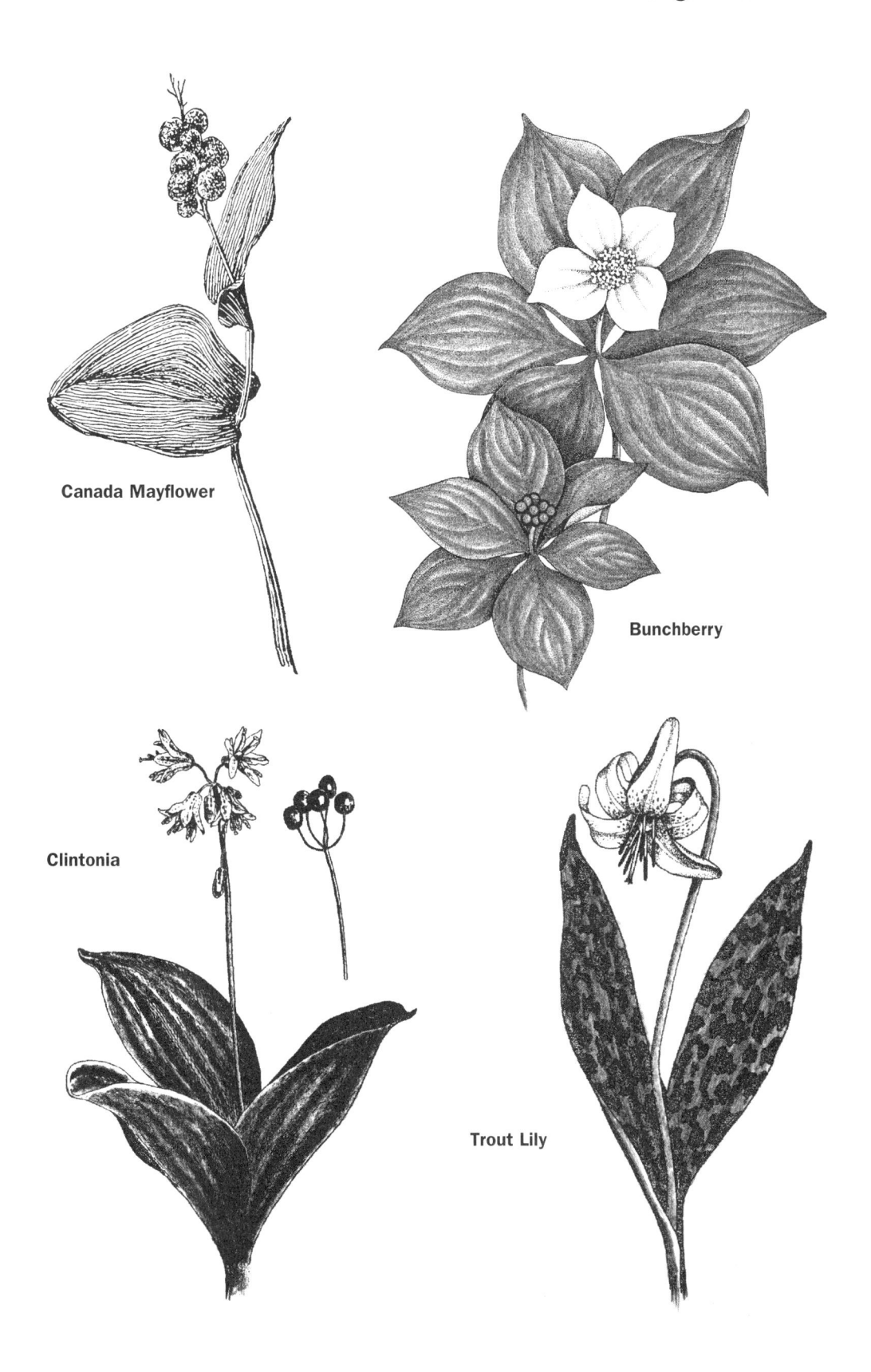

Canada Mayflower

Bunchberry

Clintonia

Trout Lily

The other major soil type is till. When an ice mass just sits there and melts on the land, like roadside snow piles in March, the mix of mineral particles dropped by the ice forms till. Till is composed of sand, silt, clay, cobbles and boulders, and veneers the land up to an elevation of about 2600 feet. It can be just a few inches thick on steep hillsides, and up to many feet deep on the lower slopes. This mix of fine and coarse mineral matter gives till a much higher nutrient level, so it can support high-demand hardwood trees like sugar maple. You can tell when you are on till just by the presence of sugar maple trees and scattered large boulders called erratics. Large boulders are too heavy to be transported by running water, therefore they are not found on outwash soils.

**Sugar Maple**

Several exceptions to these two main soil types can also be found. First, in the central Adirondacks we can find several areas of wind-deposited silt called loess (pronounced "luss"). This thin veneer of loess can be found in the "potato fields" east of Gabriels on Route 86, Upper Franklin Falls Road, and the Bear Cub Road. south of Lake Placid. The fine minerals in loess account for some of the rare decent farmlands in the central Adirondacks.

Second, in the Champlain Valley, we find heavy clay soils that are rich in nutrients but nearly impervious to water. These clay soils are deposits of fine mineral particles washed from the uplands into the freshwater lakes and saltwater sea that flooded the valley at the end of the ice age. Clay soils are the opposite of outwash sand—they percolate water slowly and confound the use of drain fields in household septic systems.

Impervious layers often develop in glacial till and outwash soils.

The Age of Ice    61

**Loess deposits** of wind-blown silt cover some places, such as the area south of Lake Placid on Bear Cub Rd. (above) and the "potato fields" near Gabriels on Route 86 (below). The fine particles created a richer soil allowing agriculture to survive.

These rust-colored "pan" layers are often composed of cemented leached iron minerals deposited several feet under the surface. Tree-root penetration through this hardpan is nearly impossible, so many trees have a shallow root zone in the soil, making them subject to wind-throw. Water, too, is slowed in its penetration of the soil, often water-logging the layer above. Hardpans can also disrupt septic system drainfields.

In the Adirondacks, as well as everywhere else, soils provide the basic support, nutrient and water reservoir for plants and animals—including humans. We use soils not only for farming but also for construction, roads and buildings. Because Adirondack soils are generally poor and the growing season short, this region was not settled on an agricultural economy as was the rest of the state. It looks different here because trees were seldom permanently cleared for farming, and a forested landscape continues to dominate the Park's character.

Very little land was cleared for farming in the central Adirondacks.

## Chapter 3  The Great North Woods

Our view of the green world around us is similar to the experience of walking down a street in a town and recognizing our friends and acquaintances. On the one hand, white pines and elms are often viewed as good friends we enjoy meeting that can be identified from a distance by their distinctive forms. On the other hand, poison ivy, though seldom found here, is always avoided once you've had experience with it. Certain flowers, such as painted trillium, are a welcome sight and a herald of spring as the sun ushers in a new season of growth and renewal.

**White Pines** are often ridgetop silhouettes in many Adirondack scenes. White Pines need sun to grow fast and are almost always the tallest trees in the forest.

## 64    Why the Adirondacks Look the Way They Do

**Elms** have the familiar feather-duster form and are common in the lower river valleys.

**Trilliums** have all their parts in three's...petals, sepals, and leaves. Purple and painted trilliums are common in the uplands, while large white trilliums are common in the Champlain Valley and southern Adirondacks.

**Red spruce**          **Black spruce**

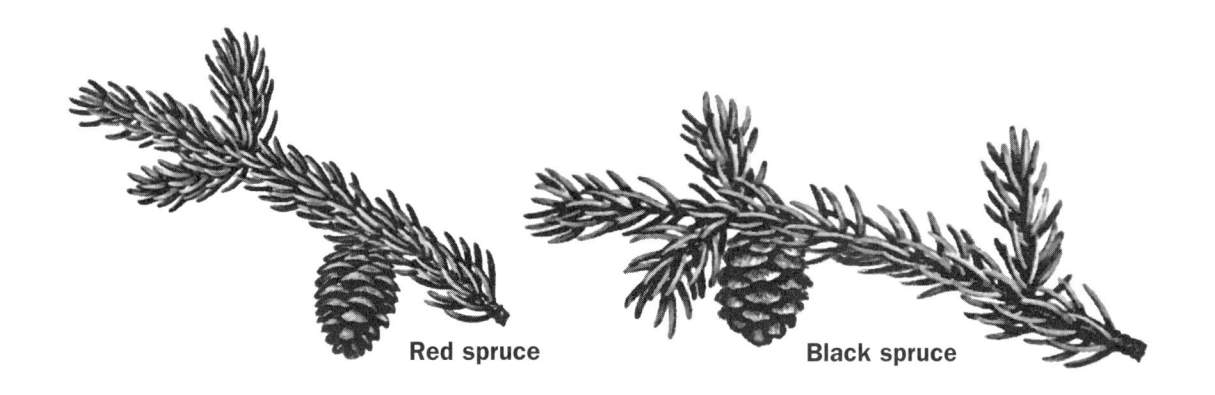

**Red spruce cones are oval** and usually about 1 1/4 " long, slightly oval. Red spruce is almost always found on dry soil. The trees can live to be 300 years old. Black Spruce is found on wet soils and bogs, and has 3/4" spherical cones.

But for most folks, the forest community is a vast city of unknown faces and personalities. This chapter will help give you some understanding of these faces and forms and perhaps give you the feeling of knowing the characters and families residing in this "town" for a long, long time.

The dominant vegetation of the Adirondacks is, of course, the many tree species comprising our forest. Although the Adirondacks are a transition zone between northern and southern forest types, in general, the central highlands are a fairly simple composition of species compared with the very complex variety of forests to the south. The Champlain Valley and the southeast fringe of the Park, lying only a few hundred feet above sea level, have representatives of the more southern forests down the Hudson Valley. Red spruce is the species that best characterizes this region, for it is represented in a wide variety of sites and occurs nowhere else in the state in such abundance. It was the last forest species to

**Red oak is common in the Champlain Valley.** It has migrated up the Ausable River Valley as far as the Cascade Lakes and Pitchoff Mountain. A few are scattered in the central Adirondacks.

## Why the Adirondacks Look the Way They Do

**Silver maple is the common hardwood** of many big river valley swamps, such as here on the Raquette River east of Tupper Lake. They survive very high ice-out floods better than other species.

migrate into the Adirondacks, arriving here only about 2,000 years ago.

Nature abhors a vacuum, so once the ice finally melted away, some 12,000 years ago, plants and animals migrated north from the ice-free south. But the near-glacial environment was tough, and only the most hearty organisms could survive. Plant pollen preserved in bottom sediments of lakes and bogs has been analyzed and reveals the sequence of how the region was re-vegetated. The first trees to invade were white spruce, preceded by other tundra plants such as dwarf birch,

# Forest Tree Pollen Time Line

| years ago | climate | events |
|---|---|---|
| present | cool moist | Today's species mix take available sites |
| 4000 | | Red Spruce arrives |
| | warm dry | Oaks dominate but then decline |
| 6000 | | Northern Hardwoods: Maple, Y. Birch, Beech arrive |
| 7500 | | Hemlock arrives |
| | | White Pine arrives |
| 9000 | | Balsam Fir, Aspen, Paper Birch arrive |
| | cold | |
| 10,500 | | White Spruce arrives |

**During the past twelve thousand years**, pollen samples have shown which trees were most abundant in response to the changing climate of the time.

mountain alder and alpine bilberry. Over the next several thousand years the climate grew progressively warmer and drier, even more so than the present, and other species soon dominated the landscape. White pine and hemlock soon invaded along with a host of hardwood trees: sugar maple, yellow birch, and American beech joined the hearty paper birch and aspens already here. During the warmest time, some 6,000 years ago, there were more red oak trees here than survive today. The climate shifted several times, but for the past 4000 years has remained fairly cool and moist. Different plant communities have evolved, depending on a given site's soil, microclimate, water and elevation. These life zones of plant and animal communities are not always evident due to natural or human-induced disturbances which will be discussed later. Also, one community often grades into another and so it combines characteristics of both. Let's take a brief look at these major life zones in the upland areas of the Park.

### Wetlands

Wetlands types often blur more than any other community but can be categorized into three major kinds. A **swamp** is any wetland with trees or shrubs in it. Hardwood swamps are usually made up of silver and red maple trees, or alders, as well as shrubs such as dogwood and winterberry. Softwood swamps are made up of white cedar, tamarack and black spruce—all conifers, or cone-bearing trees.

A **marsh** is a wetland characterized by standing water, with sedges and cattails in wet meadows, and water lilies, pickerel weed and water shield found in deep-water emergent marshes, where water is up to six feet deep. Wet meadows and shallow and deep-water marshes blend into one another depending upon the water depth. They are often caused by flooding by beavers or humans. Marshes are very productive ecosystems that nurture many forms of wonderful life in the Adirondacks, from dragonflies, fish, frogs and turtles, to bitterns, herons and ducks. Good examples of marshes can be found at the Paul Smiths VIC.

## The Great North Woods 69

**Marshes, like Heron Marsh at the Paul Smiths VIC**, is a shallow basin filled with white and yellow water lilies, pickerel weed, water shield, and many other plants. The marsh edge has a bog-like character of heath plants.

**Softwood swamps** are often on wet sand plains along rivers and lakes and are usually composed of white cedar, black spruce and balsam fir. Hemlock often is found on bouldery wet ground in ravines and lake shores.

## Marsh Life

Marshes hold a host of wildlife, from aquatic insects, frogs and turtles, to bitterns, herons, muskrats, and otters. White-tailed deer have learned to birth their fawns here to evade coyote predation.

**Spring Peepers** are tiny inch-long frogs that can be identified by the dark "X" on their back.

**Spotted Salamander**, above, and breeding red-spotted newts, below.

**The Great Blue Heron** is the largest wading bird on the marsh.

# The Great North Woods

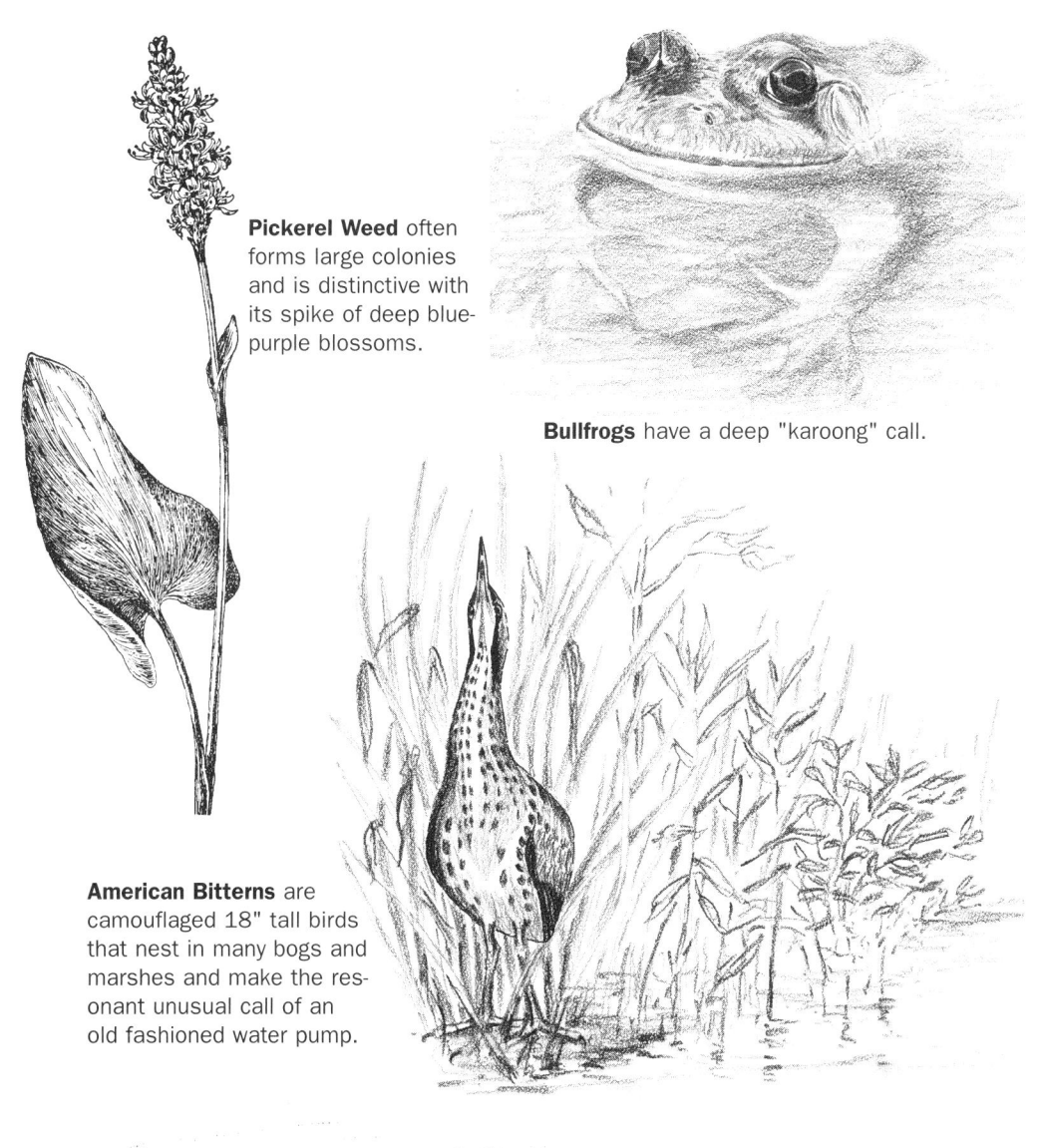

**Pickerel Weed** often forms large colonies and is distinctive with its spike of deep blue-purple blossoms.

**Bullfrogs** have a deep "karoong" call.

**American Bitterns** are camouflaged 18" tall birds that nest in many bogs and marshes and make the resonant unusual call of an old fashioned water pump.

**Painted turtles** are common residents of most Adirondack ponds and marshes, and can be seen sunning on logs and rocks.

# 72    Why the Adirondacks Look the Way They Do

**Tree Swallows** are the most common insect-eating birds on small marshes.

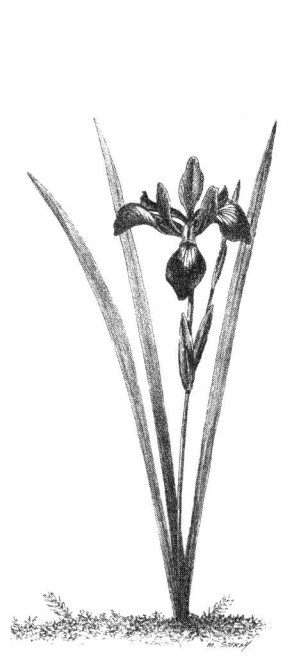

**Blue Flag, or Wild Iris**, is the big blue flower on marsh edges.

**Common Snipes** are the secretive birds that make an eerie sound over a marsh caused by air rushing through the erect outer tail feathers during a dive.

**Loons** require large areas of open water in order to take off because they are heavy birds without hollow bones.

**Broadwing Hawks** are the common medium-sized hawk that soars high over open marshlands in search of prey.

**White-throated Sparrows**' call is the distinctive, "Oh, Sweet Canada, Canada, Canada."

**Families of Common Mergansers** often have more than a dozen young to be watched over by a parent bird.

**74    Why the Adirondacks Look the Way They Do**

**Dragon fly nymphs** may take three years to mature into adulthood. On the pond bottom they are fierce predators of other aquatic organisms.

**Adult dragon flies** breed within a few weeks of adult metamorphosis.

**Kingbirds** are common flycatchers of Adirondack marshes and consume many large flying insects, including dragon flies.

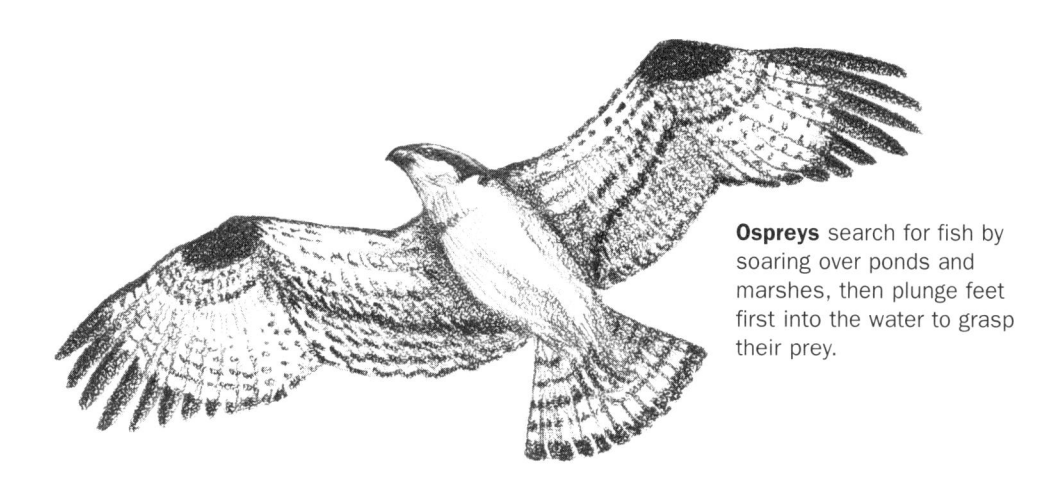

**The Great North Woods** 75

**Ospreys** search for fish by soaring over ponds and marshes, then plunge feet first into the water to grasp their prey.

**White Water Lilies** blossom later than the Yellow Water Lily; their round leaves are shaped like "packman."

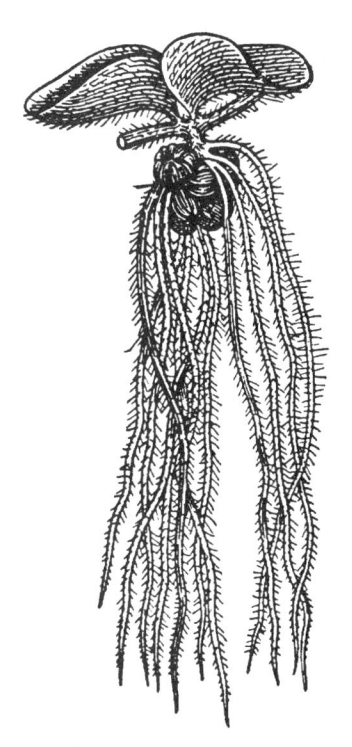

**Duckweeds** are tiny floating flowering plants that form massive bright green mats on many ponds and marshes in mid-summer.

# Why the Adirondacks Look the Way They Do

**The extensive wetland at Tupper Lake** is home to many waterfowl.

**Bogs and fens** have plants and animals adapted to acid, low- nutrient and low-oxygen environments. They are fascinating places to visit.

You can see one of the Park's largest marshes at Ausable Point at the entry point of the Ausable River into Lake Champlain. On Route 30 south of the village of Tupper Lake, where the Raquette River enters Tupper Lake, an expansive marsh has been created by the raised water of the dam on the lake's outlet.

**Bogs** are characterized by plants such as sphagnum moss, orchids and some sedges, such as cotton grass, as well as insectivorous plants such as sundews and pitcher plants. Bogs are often floating mats over low-nutrient, oxygen-depleted stagnant water in kettle holes. Bogs are uncommon outside the Adirondacks because the glacial processes that created them are seldom found elsewhere. Heath shrubs such as leatherleaf, Labrador tea, and bog rosemary are usually found in bogs. Orchid displays in the month of July are always sought out by flower lovers. At Ferd's Bog near Inlet, Silver Lake Bog, managed by the Adirondack Nature Conservancy, and at the Visitor Interpretive Center at Paul Smiths, you can access bogs easily on boardwalks. These places are enjoyable at all seasons of the year, and many uncommon boreal birds can be seen. Adirondack bogs and marshes are most abundant in the lake country north and west of the High Peaks where glacial stagnation caused pitted outwash plains and disrupted drainages over vast areas. The St. Regis Canoe Area, Spring Pond Bog, Madawaska, Massawepie Mire, and the Moose River Plains are some examples. The subregion in the northwestern quadrant of the Park is often referred to as the low-elevation Boreal Forest area.

Again, remember that there are many wetlands that exhibit characteristics of both bogs and marshes. Such places are best termed fens, where surface water moves into or through bogs bringing nutrients and oxygen to enrich the plant communities. Many lakes in the Adirondacks had small log-drive dams built on their outlets a century ago that raised the water level and created boggy fen shorelines and backwaters. Beavers occupying sites for long periods can also create similar situations. Given enough time, most bogs and fens will become forested with swamp forests of tamarack,

## Why the Adirondacks Look the Way They Do

**Bogs and Boreal communities** are most common in the northwest quadrant of the Adirondacks. Following are some of the places and community members you are likely to witness during an excursion into one of these areas.

**October brings golden color** of tamaracks and seed heads of cotton grass, as here on Barnum Pond Outlet at the Paul Smiths VIC.

**Snowberry** is the low creeping ground cover plant at the edge of boreal forest and bog mat. The white berry has a sweet wintergreen flavor.

**Black Spruce** is the small tree that carries its live branches in small bunches at the top of the tree. Black Spruces spread in clusters of vegetative clones as lower branches get pushed into sphagnum surfaces and take root.

## The Great North Woods    79

**Pitcher Plants** are insectivorous bog plants that capture insects in its water-filled hollow leaves. The round magenta flowers are seen throughout summer.

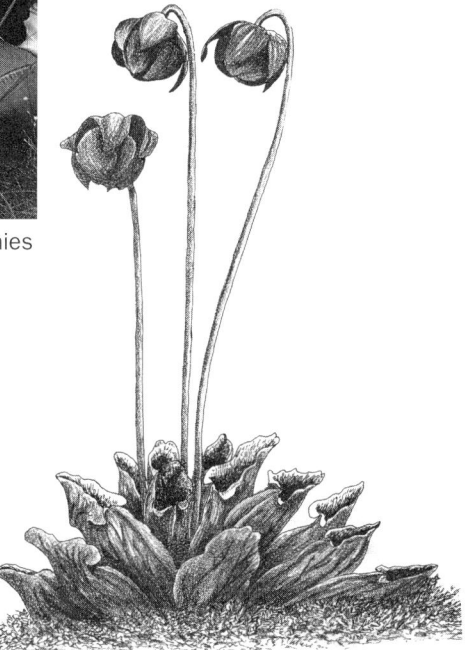

**Bladderwort** is a short, yellow-blossomed plant that grows in colonies in open shallow water of many bogs.

**Cranberry** is a small creeping bog plant whose fruit is edible in late autumn or early the following spring after seasoning during the winter.

**Labrador Tea** has white blossoms and leaves that are densely fuzzy on the underside of the rolled leaf.

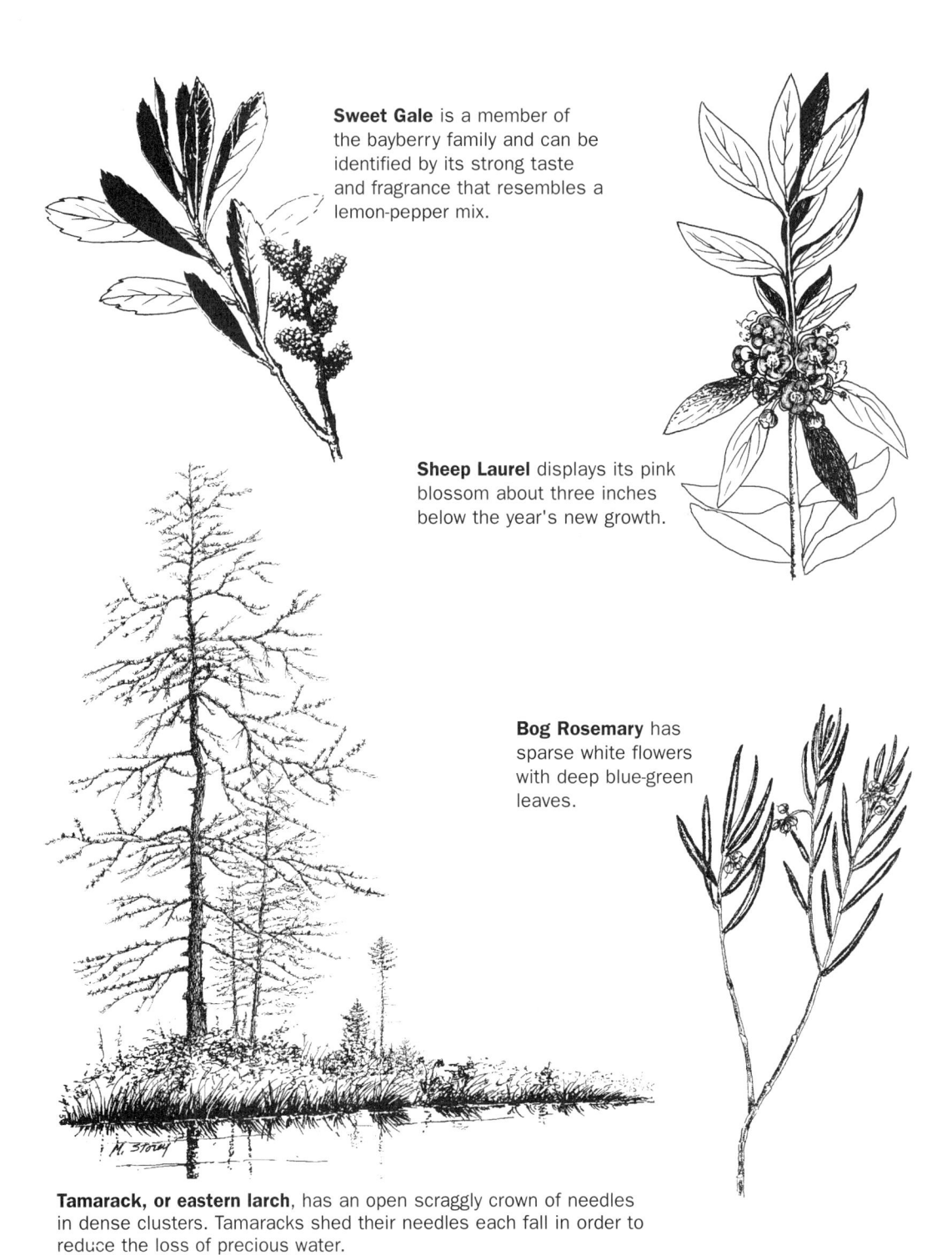

# 80   Why the Adirondacks Look the Way They Do

**Sweet Gale** is a member of the bayberry family and can be identified by its strong taste and fragrance that resembles a lemon-pepper mix.

**Sheep Laurel** displays its pink blossom about three inches below the year's new growth.

**Bog Rosemary** has sparse white flowers with deep blue-green leaves.

**Tamarack, or eastern larch**, has an open scraggly crown of needles in dense clusters. Tamaracks shed their needles each fall in order to reduce the loss of precious water.

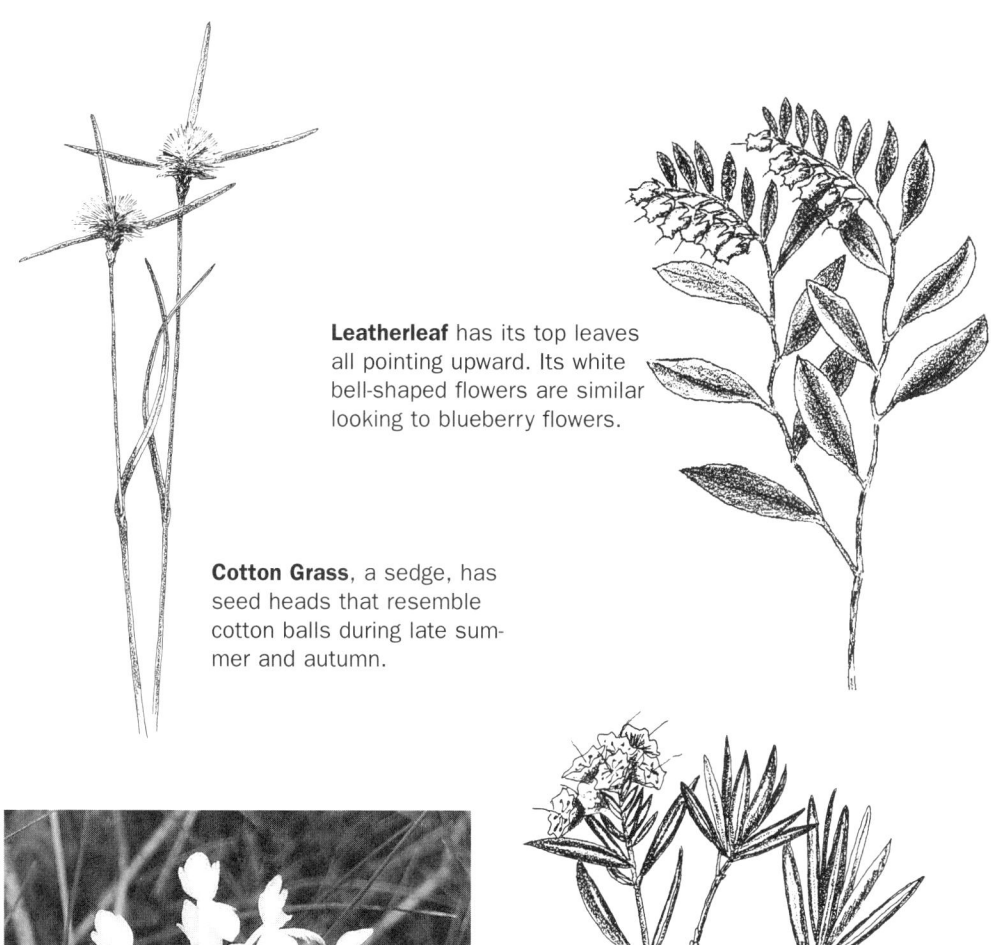

**The Great North Woods** 81

**Leatherleaf** has its top leaves all pointing upward. Its white bell-shaped flowers are similar looking to blueberry flowers.

**Cotton Grass**, a sedge, has seed heads that resemble cotton balls during late summer and autumn.

**Bog Laurel** is the pink-flowered shrub that displays its blossom at the very top of the new growth.

**White-fringed Orchis** is a ten-inch orchid very common in most Adirondack bogs.

## Boreal Birds

**Hawk Owls** often migrate into boggy Adirondack habitats during mid-winter.

**Spruce Grouse** are very rare boreal birds found in only a few northwest regional bogs.

**The Great North Woods**   83

**Black-backed Woodpeckers** search for insects by gently flaking the bark from red and black spruces.

**Gray Jays** are curious nervous birds that are most commonly seen in late autumn in many Adirondack boreal communities

**Boreal Chickadees** are uncommon birds that have a brown head and call with a "wheezy" song compared to the more familiar Black-capped Chickadee.

### 84   Why the Adirondacks Look the Way They Do

**Lake Champlain** is home to a variety of wildlife not commonly found in the uplands of the Adirondacks. Here we find cormorants, large great blue heron rookeries, and large flocks of Canada geese.

**A long-time beaver pond habitat,** this stream and pond near Floodwood Mountain contains organisms found in bogs, fens and marshes.

black spruce and northern white cedar. This occurs as peat deposits build up beneath the floating mat, creating a more solid support for trees.

Soil moisture governs what species of trees will grow in the valleys. Since the mineral soil is composed of low-nutrient sand and gravel with little silt and clay content, only the hardiest plants survive. On wet soils, a forest of balsam fir, black spruce and tamarack will eventually claim the site. The ground cover will be composed of mosses, ferns and sphagnum. On drier soils, a forest of red spruce, balsam fir, red maple, yellow birch, and hemlock will claim this "mixed wood" forest. An understory of witchhobble will be common here, as well as a variety of wildflowers such as trillium and bunchberry.

One exception to this scheme is the large, very sandy outwash areas of the southwest and southeast corners of the Park. Here, the sandy

# 86    Why the Adirondacks Look the Way They Do

**There are 30,000 miles of brooks**, rivers and streams in the Adirondack Park, with habitats that host a great variety of life.

**Hemlocks can live to be 650** years old in the Adirondacks. This old-growth specimen is on Paul Smiths College property.

droughty soils allow white pine to compete best. The nature trail at Pack Demonstration Forest north of Warrensburg gives visitors the chance to experience a virgin forest of white pine, spruce and hemlock, some of which are known to be more than three hundred years old. White pine, being shade-intolerant, grows best in full sunlight. Therefore it is a "catastrophe species"—meaning it often grows on sites opened up by a major disturbance such as fire or windstorm. All trees grow up at the same time, with no shade to hinder them.

# 88   Why the Adirondacks Look the Way They Do

**You can visit hemlock groves** on the Boreal Life Trail at the Paul Smiths Visitor Interpretive Center.

**Spruce, Fir and Pine** are often regenerated by major disturbances such as fire, wind or heavy logging. As the thousands of young trees grow up together, competition thins the stand, leaving only a handful of older trees.

**Old-Growth hardwoods**, such as this sugar maple, have a distinct "stag head" form that signifies their advanced age.

Nearly 60 percent of the Park is covered with northern hardwood forest. This forest type occurs on slopes from 1,400 to 2,600 feet in elevation, the zone of deposited glacial till soil. Glacial till contains a larger percentage of clay and silt-size particles that feed the most nutrient-demanding species. One of most demanding is sugar maple. Indeed, if you see a sugar maple, you can almost be sure you are on till soil. Other species mix in to make this forest community: beech, yellow birch, red spruce and hemlock, with white ash, hophornbeam and basswood represented on the very richest soils. This is the forest that gives the Park the fantastic fall colors starting in mid-September and ending in mid-October.

Above 2,600 feet the glacial till begins to run out, and a poorer, organic soil begins. This is because the glacial ice contained little in the way of minerals above this elevation. As the ice melted, a veneer of mineral soil was dropped over the bedrock. At higher elevations, there simply wasn't as much source material to make mineral soil. So, the slopes above 2,800 feet are largely clothed in an evergreen

**The Bicknell's thrush and juncos** are birds of the subalpine zone during the summer. The thrushes migrate south, while the juncos retreat to local lower elevations for the winter.

**Wind-blown ice crystals** shave the tops off unprotected trees during the harsh winters. Trees can only grow as tall as the snow depth.

forest of balsam fir and red spruce, developed on a largely organic soil. At about 3500 feet the forest begins to shrink in height as growing conditions get tougher, and black spruce replaces red spruce. Higher up, the trees cannot grow any taller than the normal snow depth. During winter, snow acts as an insulator and protects trees from wind-driven ice crystals that continually abrade any branches and leaders exposed above the snow depth.

**Aliens in the Adirondacks:** Flowers of European origin are found throughout the Park. Open field flowers such as daisies, hawkweeds and St. Johnswort are the most common aliens, but deep woods invaders such as helleborine are increasing.

Less than 100 acres in the entire six million acre Adirondack Park are classified as alpine—above timberline. They are mountaintop islands of flora that colonized the peaks shortly after deglaciation some 12,000 years ago. In a curious twist, many of the hardiest plants on mountaintops are the same plants that colonize bogs and fens on the valley floors. There is a reason for this: the conditions are so difficult in both places that only hardy plants can survive in both places. Every nook and cranny, any hollow and lee, is a shelter for plants and animals that helps them survive the relentless winds that sweep the highest peaks. This zone of life is a very tough and delicate place to eke out a living, so if you climb above timberline, stick to the open rock and do not walk or sit on any of the plants. Valiant efforts have been made by volunteers to stabilize and rehabilitate areas trampled by thoughtless hikers.

Ecologists have studied and can predict just about everything that might influence the sorting out of plant communities from valley to mountaintop. But nature is seldom so simple or static. There is a flow of energy in time and space with so many dynamic twists that things never quite fit the perfect descriptions that were just set out. Why is it that this place that you are looking at seems a little different from those neat pigeon-hole descriptions ecologists like to label as communities? The following chapter will take a look at these forces that shape the Adirondack scenery into a myriad of natural nuances that fit a time-lapse video better than the snapshot view we are usually given.

**Sweetfern** is the common ground plant of the pitch pine barrens community. It is very fragrant and can be savored from a great distance.

# Zones of Adirondack Life

The diagram below describes the major life zones of most of the Adirondacks that you are likely to see while traveling here. On the east side, in the near-sea level Champlain Valley, the climate is warmer and drier, and forests of oak and pitch pine are common. But on most of the upland plateau, valley bottoms average 1600 feet above sea level and mountain tops reach above a mile. The Park is also the meeting ground of northern boreal forest and the rich hardwood forests to the south. Nearly 15% of the Adirondack Park is wetland or water surface, painting a rich tapestry of habitats.

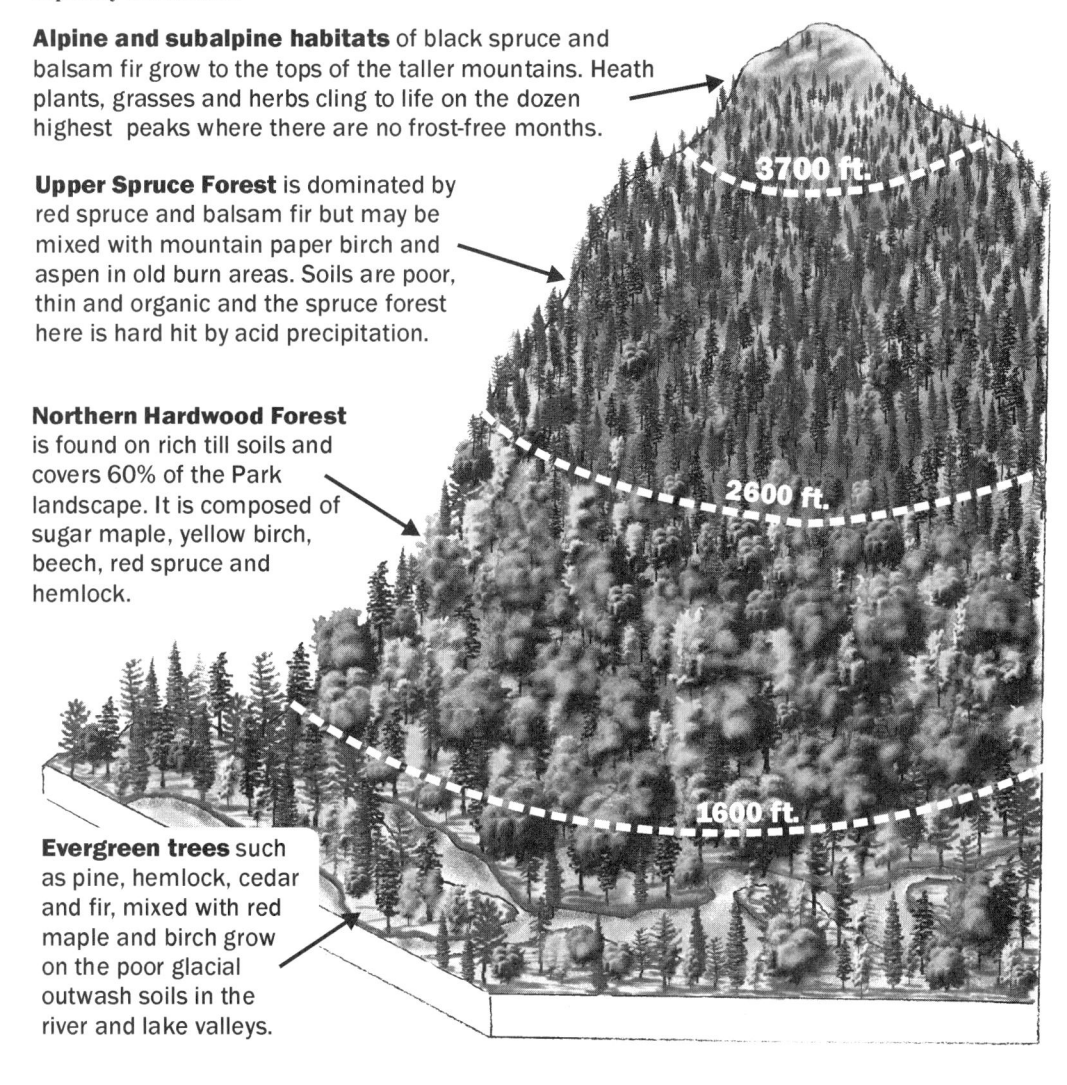

**Alpine and subalpine habitats** of black spruce and balsam fir grow to the tops of the taller mountains. Heath plants, grasses and herbs cling to life on the dozen highest peaks where there are no frost-free months.

**Upper Spruce Forest** is dominated by red spruce and balsam fir but may be mixed with mountain paper birch and aspen in old burn areas. Soils are poor, thin and organic and the spruce forest here is hard hit by acid precipitation.

**Northern Hardwood Forest** is found on rich till soils and covers 60% of the Park landscape. It is composed of sugar maple, yellow birch, beech, red spruce and hemlock.

**Evergreen trees** such as pine, hemlock, cedar and fir, mixed with red maple and birch grow on the poor glacial outwash soils in the river and lake valleys.

## Why the Adirondacks Look the Way They Do

**White cedar** is one of few evergreen trees that can sprout from a cut stump. You can find clumps of white cedars along many lake shores, like these at the Newcomb VIC.

**White-tailed deer** walk along lake shores on the ice and browse cedars, creating a neatly trimmed line.

## 96   Why the Adirondacks Look the Way They Do

**You won't find whole balsam fir cones**, because they disintegrate in late summer, releasing the seeds and scales to the wind. Only the central spike remains on the tree.

**Red pines have very thin**, open crowns that stand up to wind and snow loads better than white pine, so you can find them on windy island sites and shore lines. In the bottom photo, the red pines are marked "X" and the white pines "O".

# The Great North Woods

**Billows of foam float** on many of the Lake Country streams because they flow from bogs and fens where tannic acids create the tea-colored water. Tannic acids strengthen surface film in the water that holds foamy bubbles for a long time. Many shorelines, and pools below waterfalls, display foamy piles, as here at Gleason's Falls on the Grass River.

**Fishing Brook dam**, just off Rt. 28N, was built as an early log-drive dam to float logs to the Hudson River.

**Some old burn areas** in the north-central Adirondacks have luxuriant colonies of Hay-scented Ferns. The dense growth chokes out most tree and shrub regeneration, hence a pure ground cover of this single aggressive specie.

**Red-eyed Vireos** are the summer songsters in the mixed forests of the Adirondacks. Their incessant song sounds like, "Where am I... here I am... in a tree."

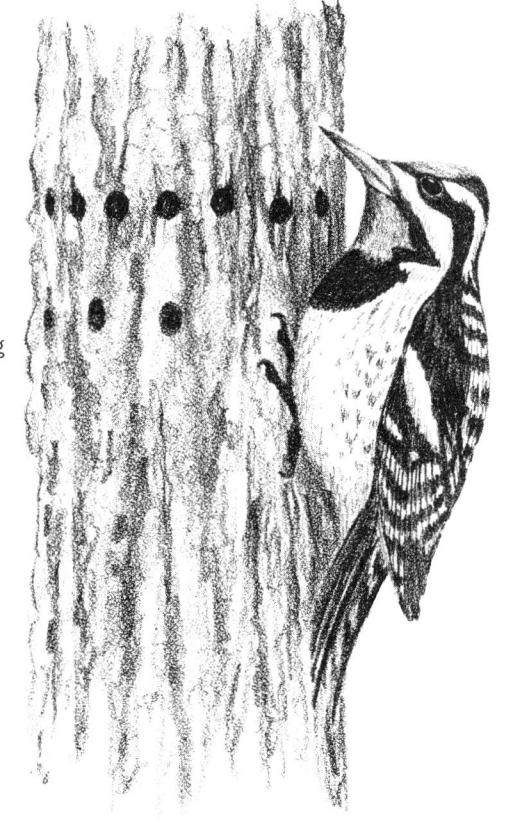

**Yellow-bellied Sapsuckers** create the strings of horizontal 1/4 inch diameter holes that are especially common in hemlocks and paper birch trees. The birds feed on tiny insects that are attracted to the sap that oozes into the holes.

**Yellow-bellied Sapsuckers** are common birds in the mature aspen forests that resulted from the fires of the early 1900's, nesting in cavities created by pileated and hairy woodpeckers.

**Ovenbirds** are the common warbler of hardwood forests that sing in late Spring, "Teacher-teacher-teacher," as they establish breeding territory.

# The Great North Woods 101

**Sharp-shinned Hawks** are the common small hawk of the Adirondacks that feeds mostly on song birds. During winter, they often hunt the birds attracted to backyard bird feeding stations.

**Hermit Thrushes** sing in early summer with a soft flute-like song.

**Piliated Woodpeckers** are the crow-sized bird with the red crest that chisel the large rectangular holes in trees. The birds are searching for carpenter ants inside the tree, which they locate by listening for the chewing sounds of ants. Balsam fir trees are often colonized by ants in the lower six feet of trunk and piliateds feed heavily on them.

## Chapter 4   Reading the Landscape

The previous chapter described how nature would organize life in the Adirondacks if there were no humans, severe weather or other major alterations brought by fire, insects, disease or wildlife influences. The history of the Adirondacks over the past 200 years has been anything but neat. The region has gone from a totally wild place to totally disrupted to wildness reborn. At the beginning of the 21st century, the Adirondacks are in a state of healing and renewal following a time of drastic changes, forest destruction, wildlife obliteration and exotic species introduction that started more than a century and a half ago. The following pages will describe what you see on this landscape now and why it looks the way it does.

### Beavers

When you drive along the back roads and highways of the Park, you are struck by the many flooded dead-tree hollows in view. Some are filled

**Beaver Lodge** at pond edge.

**Panther Mountain flow** is a long-term beaver habitat that is continually reflooded and occupied by beavers.

with water, some are dry, but all are in a state of change. The cause will be evident if you spot the dome-shaped pile of sticks back along the shore. You see their work everywhere, from the smallest ponds and streams to the largest Adirondack lakes.

Beaver populations exploded starting in the 1970s when protests disrupted the fur industry and beaver pelt prices plummeted. It was no longer fashionable for people to wear another animal's fur. Trappers stopped trapping beavers, and their populations began expanding into every possible place that they could colonize. Beavers are territorial, and instinct limits the number of individuals on smaller waterbodies to just one family (usually two to seven animals) at any given time. Offspring at age one and a half are forced to strike out and find their own territory

**Beavers feed** on lush, nutritious green plants during summer and fall. Where the rich rhizomes of water lilies can be found, beavers feed on them all fall and winter because they are far more nutritious than the inner bark of trees.

and mate. No staying back home with mom and dad when the good job doesn't come along after college graduation! Every autumn there is a mad rush by young beavers to find unoccupied habitat, build a dam and lodge and get ready for winter. Many don't make it, and as new territories became scarcer, the more distant the new homemakers have to travel.

Beavers were nearly extirpated from the Adirondacks by 1900, when trapping bans went into effect, and attempts were spurred to bring them back. At that time, destructive forest fires swept hundreds of thousands of acres of forest, including many miles of Adirondack lake and river shorelines. The forest grew back quickly and was made up of a pioneer forest composed largely of aspen, paper birch and white pine. The inner bark of aspen and paper birch are favorite fall and winter food of beavers, but since there were no beavers here at that time, those trees grew to maturity. We still see these shoreline forests throughout the Park. Beaver populations slowly recovered, and trapping was again allowed by 1930. At the present time, wolves and mountain lions are rare, so beavers have no population control other than habitat availability, road kills, or modest human trapping. Beavers sense when territory is no longer available and may stop breeding for several years—a most natural form of birth control that humans might emulate.

As the lack of beavers influenced the forest of a century ago, the renewed population of beavers now has, and will continue to have, a great influence on wetlands, waterways and shorelines of the Park. A brief glimpse in time may help interpret this situation. In 1986, I began designing the trail systems at the two Visitor Interpretive Centers at Paul Smiths and Newcomb. The two sites were very different. Paul Smiths had large wetlands, bogs, ponds and streams in a glacial outwash area. The land had been burned in 1912, and much of the forest was composed of pioneer species about seventy years old. The marsh hosted a single beaver colony that had moved into the pond several years earlier.

The visitor center at Newcomb was on a mile-long peninsula jutting out into Rich Lake. The forest was on glacial till, almost virgin Northern hardwoods and shoreline cedars, with a small cobble-bottomed stream entering the larger river outlet. No beaver activity was observed there as I began flagging the routes of the three trails in the summer of 1987. When I returned to oversee the trail construction in April of 1988, I found Little Sucker Brook dammed in three locations right where I planned to cross it. The interpretive plan changed from trout habitat to beaver influence, and plan B was launched. Four years later, the beavers abandoned the site, the dams washed out, and the stream returned to a babbling brook. But for many years to come those little pond sites will be a very different habitat from what they once were. The flooded dead

**Young beavers** often move into unoccupied small drainages that have limited habitat, like this small stream at the Newcomb VIC. The colony only lasted three years and was then abandoned. The same area was re-occupied ten years later for another short cycle.

trees are woodpecker heaven; the sunlight hitting the forest floor has sparked an explosion of new plant and animal life not possible in the dense shade of the original forest. Species of songbirds and other animals will be present on that site for many years that would be absent in an undisturbed forest.

At Paul Smiths, the Barnum Brook Trail was built through an eighty year old forest of paper birch and aspen, with an understory of balsam fir. Very little beaver feeding was noted along the marsh shoreline. Then, starting in the winter of 1994, beaver feeding activity exploded on the site. It was a very tough winter of deep snow and exceptionally cold temperatures. Beavers wallowed through the thirty inches of snow and chewed down more than forty aspen and paper birches, clipping off the smaller branches and dragging them to shoreline holes in the ice. Over the next

**The second flooding** of Little Sucker Brook site at the Newcomb VIC showed a new beaver occupation that surely will be a short term colony in this small food-starved habitat.

# 110   Why the Adirondacks Look the Way They Do

**The original second-growth forest** of paper birch and aspen along the Barnum Brook Trail at the Paul Smiths VIC when it was designed in 1987.

**Beavers cut nearly every aspen** and paper birch during the winter of 1994.

several years, the colony continued its fall and winter feeding of aspen and birch and ended up eliminating just about all those species, leaving an evergreen forest in their place. The forest there will be very different for the next millennia because of beaver activity on that site. On the marsh, the beavers moved, built new lodges and rebuilt old ones at least five times in the fourteen years that I observed them.

Beavers are creating thousands of these disturbances every year throughout the Adirondacks. People often become perturbed when their dams flood trails and roads. Beavers relish the inner bark of aspen and paper birch but will eat the inner bark of many other species of hardwoods, such as beech, ash, alder and yellow birch. They do not like the bark of red maple and most evergreen trees, though they may chew them down for the construction of dams and lodges, but seldom eat those

## 112   Why the Adirondacks Look the Way They Do

**Beavers are active all winter,** feeding on shoreline tree bark, cached sticks and lily roots.

**This heavily forested area** just east of Saranac Lake on Rt 86 was flooded by a shallow beaver dam for less than six months. All the trees died, creating a transitional forest of aspen and paper birch. The image was taken twelve years after the flooding.

**A small flooded and abandoned** beaver pond along the Raquette Falls Trail south of Corey's. Sites like this are often recolonized by beavers every few years.

species' bark. What does this mean for the future? Most shorelines now lined with aspen, paper birch and other hardwoods will be stripped of those trees and replaced by pine, balsam, cedar, spruce and hemlock. A century from now, the Park's shorelines will be very different from what we still see today if beaver populations stay elevated.

## Mariah

Of all the forces that shape the forest landscape, wind is by far the most devastating and rapid. Early maps of the Adirondacks noted blowdowns in several places, especially the swath of downed trees in the north-central part of the Park dated 1845. In recent times, two major storms have swept the Adirondacks—the first on Thanksgiving Day 1950 and the second on July 15, 1995.

## 114   Why the Adirondacks Look the Way They Do

**Shallow rooting** of trees in Adirondack soil contributes to easy windthrow.

**Windthrow creates a hummock and hollow** landscape in a forested environment. The roots carry soil and rocks to a pile adjacent to where the living roots were.

**Notice the rocks and soil** still held in this old windthrow.

The 1950 storm was a classic late-season "nor'easter," blowing in off the mid-Atlantic from the east and smashing the south-central Adirondacks with sustained winds of well over one hundred miles an hour, toppling countless trees. It was deer season, and hundreds of hunters were deep in the woods as the storm raged. Adirondack trees are especially vulnerable to winds from the east; they are braced for the prevailing winds which come from the south and west. Conservation Department surveys later determined that as many as 400,000 acres of forest was destroyed during the day long storm. State foresters at the time knew little about managing the wild lands of the state Forest Preserve, so the department, worried about fire danger, closed the affected region to

# Why the Adirondacks Look the Way They Do

**An old hemlock trunk** that remained from the 1950 blowdown is still easily identified along the trail to Raquette Falls.

**Old growth forest** along the trail to Raquette Falls.

**An old yellow birch** was tilted over in the 1950 blowdown, and its upper branches became multiple trunks.

## Why the Adirondacks Look the Way They Do

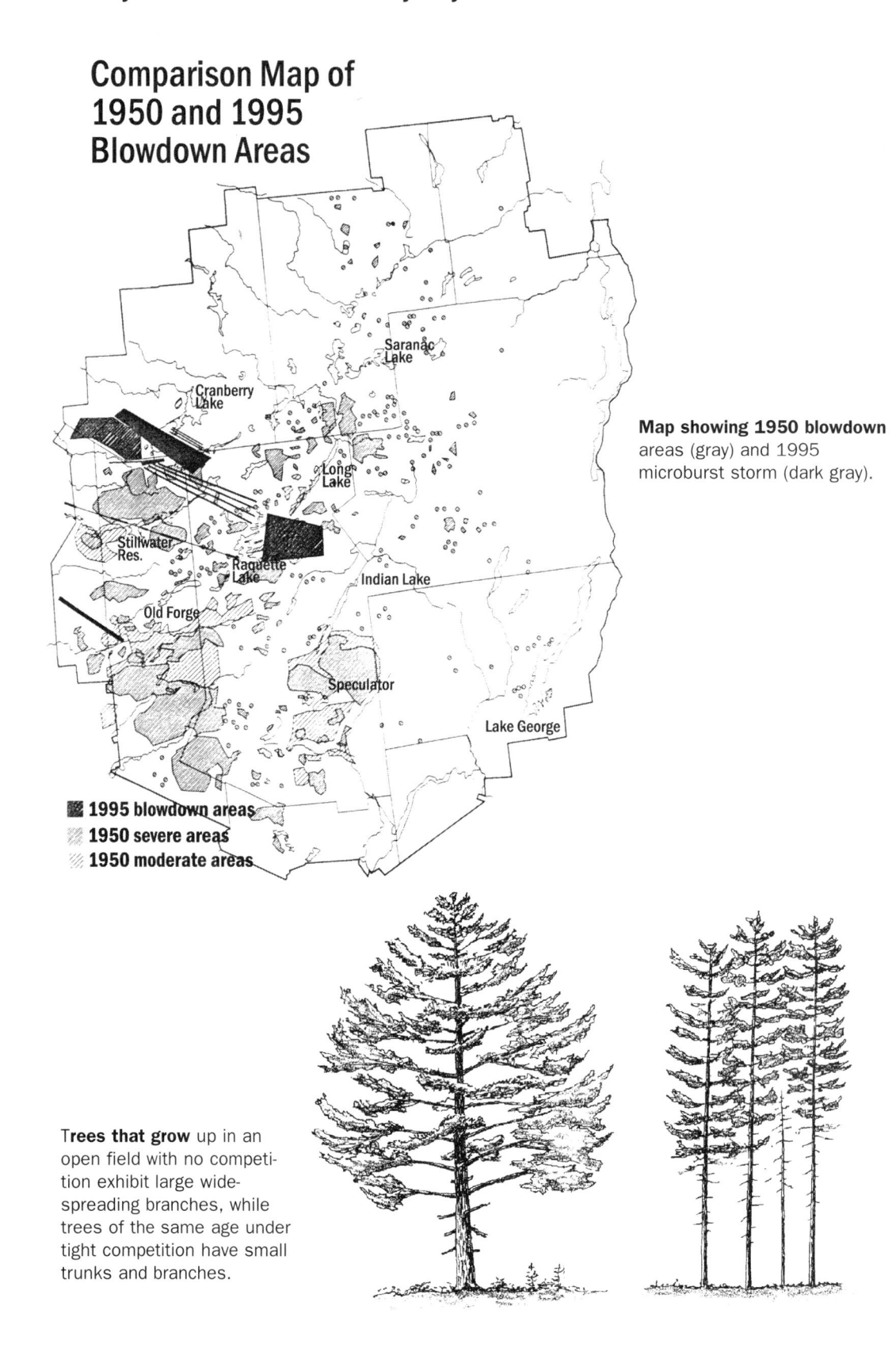

### Comparison Map of 1950 and 1995 Blowdown Areas

**Map showing 1950 blowdown** areas (gray) and 1995 microburst storm (dark gray).

■ 1995 blowdown areas
▨ 1950 severe areas
▧ 1950 moderate areas

**Trees that grow** up in an open field with no competition exhibit large wide-spreading branches, while trees of the same age under tight competition have small trunks and branches.

recreational uses and allowed "salvage" logging to clean the woods of all the downed and damaged trees. This was the only time in the history of the Forest Preserve that logging was ever permitted without an amendment to the State Constitution. Hundreds of truck trails were built into virgin territory to extract the logs. Salvage operations lasted for more than four years.

On a hike in the forest, you can still see signs of the 1950 blowdown. Look on the ground for old moss-covered trunks of hemlocks, often in clusters, especially in old-growth areas on Forest Preserve land. An example would be the trail into Ampersand Mountain and Middle Saranac Lake beach, about eight miles west of Saranac Lake village on Route 3. That land, in state ownership since 1870, had never been logged until the blowdown. There are still huge sugar maples and yellow birches living in that forest that exceed 300 years old. Many old hemlocks were blown over but were left in the forest because of the low value of the wood. It often takes well over a century for nature to recycle a stump or log lying on the ground and turn it into soil, so downed trees of the 1950 storm are still in evidence. White pine stumps and trunks often last much longer because of the higher resin content that deters fungus and insect attack.

Unlike the Great Blowdown of 1950, the storm of 1995 was caused by a line of intense thunderstorms moving at high speed, originating in southern Ontario and blasting into the Adirondacks from the northwest. It happened early in the morning, just before dawn on July 15th, and there were thousands of campers in the woods on that summer day.

A close friend and his wife were camped on the south shore of Lake Lila when the storm hit. They thought it was a tornado as the winds blasted the giant white pines around them, shearing them off like cut grass and hurling them to the ground. The terrified couple huddled in their tent for several minutes. When the crashing stopped, an eerie silence fell as dawn broke. State campgrounds at Piseco and Lake Eaton were hit, as well as back-country tracts like Lake Lila and the Five Ponds Wilderness. Several people lost their lives to falling trees, and hundreds of homes sustained damage.

The devastation occurred across the north-central Adirondacks, all the way to Schroon Lake. The massive storm was called a "microburst," a front made of a line of powerful cumulo-nimbus clouds that produced tremendous down drafts reaching 200 miles per hour, smashing into the ground and spreading in all directions. Curiously, the storm took the same path as the 1845 wind storm, according to early maps.

You can see the results of the 1995 storm in many backcountry locations as well as from the roadside. On Route 30, about three miles north of Long Lake, the best example of the destruction is easily viewed. A balsam fir and red spruce forest about one hundred years old was blasted by the storm; trees were sheared off about twenty feet above the ground, or were entirely uprooted. The day after the storm it looked like a giant hedge-trimmer had evenly clipped the entire forest. Not one tree survived the onslaught. I happened to drive through the area the day after the microburst, and the utter devastation remains vivid in my memory.

Much more research was done on this storm than the one in 1950. Meteorological developments and sequences were analyzed. Sites of heavy and light destruction were precisely mapped and analyzed by teams of ecologists and foresters. Policymakers were given scientific reports based on facts rather than conjecture so that proper management schemes were developed in relation to the resources and land classifications of the affected areas. Permits were issued for private lands so that

**Photo of 1995 Blowdown** about three miles north of Long Lake on Route 30. Photo was taken seven years after the storm.

# Trees in Tough Places

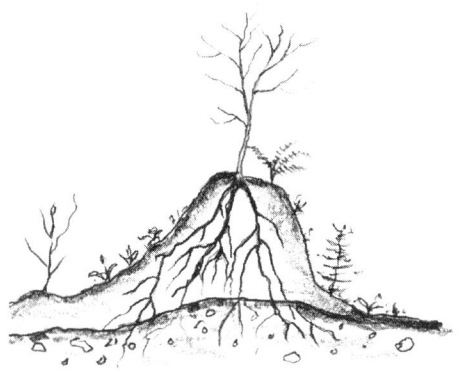

**Eighty year sequence** of a birch tree growing on a rotting stump, eventually developing stilt trunks as the roots are exposed to air.

**Sisters on the rocks,** yellow birch and hemlocks, are the most common species of trees to colonize boulder tops because their seeds germinate and grow in rotting wood covering the surface.

**Yellow birch** on stilts.

## 122   Why the Adirondacks Look the Way They Do

**Illustration of fifty year sequence** of hemlock and yellow birch growing on rotting log resting on a rock.

**Hemlock** on boulder.

**Shoreline and beach ridges** are created by windthrown trees that carry and pile soil and rocks in their overturned roots during centuries of storms.

salvage cleanup and regeneration cuts could be completed as soon as possible. On state Forest Preserve lands, no salvage logging was allowed in either Wild Forest or Wilderness areas, and the downed trees were left to rot slowly in place. The Adirondacks luckily had a normal wet summer in both 1995 and 1996, so no wildfires erupted in fuel-rich areas. Nature is already on its healing process.

Some of the hardest hit areas were old-growth lands in the northwestern Adirondacks. In the Five Ponds Wilderness Area southwest of Cranberry Lake many trees averaging 250 to 350 years old were flattened or sheared off. Old-growth areas around Raquette Lake and Eagle Bay were touched in a more spotty fashion. After five years, the impact was hardly noticeable in most areas of the Park. Smaller localized microburst storms occur in the Adirondacks every summer when powerful thunderstorms build in the humid air coming off Lake Ontario and pop up in the mountains.

### Forest on the Wing

Whether the disturbance is caused by small or widespread storms, nature responds to heal the damage as soon as it occurs. Big storms disturb large areas of forest, wiping out shade-producing tree canopies that allow sunlight to penetrate to the ground. Hidden just below the leaf litter of the previous year are countless seeds just waiting for the solar energy to trip their germination trigger. In most circumstances, birds are the peddlers of this forest opulence. Forest-dwelling birds feed on insects when raising young, but as the summer continues, they feed on the abundance of berries, seeds and fruits of trees and shrubs in the canopy and forest edges. Raspberries, blueberries, black and pin cherries, and numerous viburnum seeds are relished fruits. The seeds pass unaffected through the birds' digestive tracts and fall to the ground, where they soon are covered by autumn leaves and safely buried. They may sit there in the shade for a century or more waiting for the sun's warmth to set them off.

Light wind-blown seeds of aspen, fireweed and milkweed may also blow in from many miles away, ready to colonize any site with adequate sunlight. Thus, the nature of the Adirondacks has a plan to retake any site that is disturbed or opened up in any way. Wings and wind play the critical role in this healing process.

Smaller disturbed areas are reactive in other ways. When a single tree falls, more sunlight reaches the forest floor and understory vegetation. Small trees may extend adjacent branches into the opening. Root sprouts may erupt and send up young trees. Shade-tolerant trees may rapidly add new growth because of the additional solar energy. Small trees like striped maple, mountain maple and mountain ash may germinate seeds and fill in the little opening.

In a related matter, many shorelines of larger lakes and ponds often exhibit a low ridge adjacent to the water or beach, sometimes reaching a height of six feet and vegetated with pines and hemlocks. These ridges are formed by wind toppling the large trees growing there. As the tree is overturned, sand and gravel is trapped in the root system and mounded in a new location slightly inland. Over dozens of centuries, this disturbance is repeated many times and a taller ridge is built.

Native red pines are not common in the Adirondack forest, but they are common on many islands of the larger lakes, such as Lower Saranac Lake. Research has shown that red pines are successful in colonizing these sites because their open crowns tolerate the constant buffeting of winds and shed the heavy snow loads that topple white pines, balsam fir, and hemlock on these exposed sites.

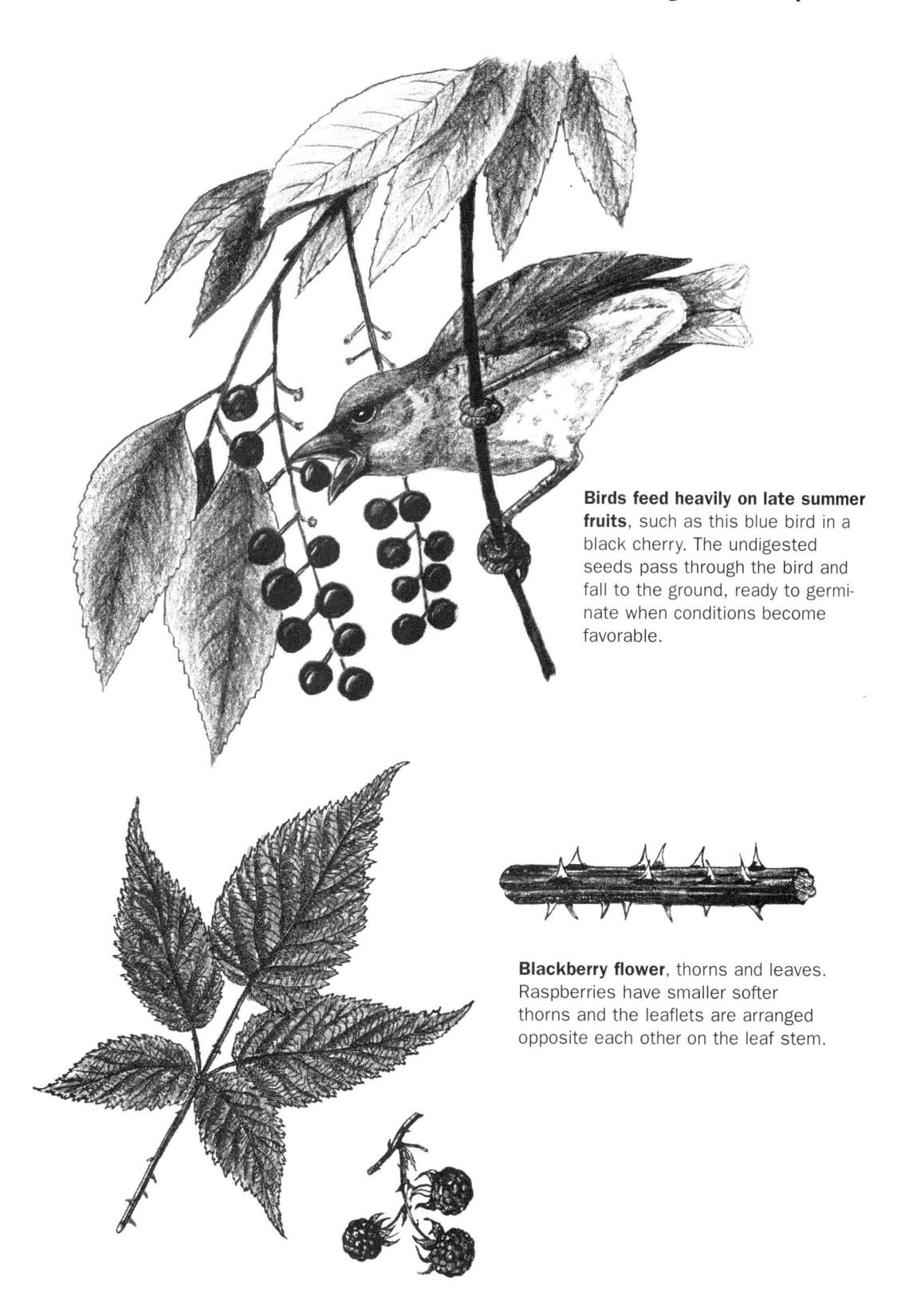

**Birds feed heavily on late summer fruits**, such as this blue bird in a black cherry. The undigested seeds pass through the bird and fall to the ground, ready to germinate when conditions become favorable.

**Blackberry flower**, thorns and leaves. Raspberries have smaller softer thorns and the leaflets are arranged opposite each other on the leaf stem.

## 126    Why the Adirondacks Look the Way They Do

**Chokecherry** blossoms and leaves.

**Shadbush**, also known as Serviceberry, is one of the first flowring shrubs to bloom in the Spring.

**Pin Cherry, Black Cherry, Chokecherry and Shadbush** are the common small trees of the forest edge. All have showy white blossoms.

**Cedar Waxwings** are the handsome birds widely known to feed on the many tree and shrub fruits of the Adirondack forest.

## Reading the Landscape 127

**Catbirds** are common in the Champlain Valley and Southern Adirondacks. They often feed in thickets of wild raisin, as pictured here.

**Pale orange hairs** along the mid-rib of a Black Cherry leaf help to identify this tree from other cherry trees.

**Witch-hobble** is the common understory shrub of Adirondack hardwood forests. The flowers blossom in concentric circles and eventually produce a bright red fruit in early autumn.

**Bunchberries** are members of the dogwood family and have showy white flowers. They produce red fruit in autumn that are edible, but taste like cardboard.

**Witch-hobble** is also known as buckbrush because the naked bud scales of autumn resemble the velvet-covered antlers of a deer.

## Why the Adirondacks Look the Way They Do

**Almost all communities in the Adirondacks** started as mill towns, originating on sites where water-power could be exploited to run saw mills.

**Rivers were declared public highways** in the 1800's and millions of trees were cut and floated to mills throughout the Adirondacks.

**Small log-drive dams** were built on smaller streams in late fall. Water backed up and logs were stacked on the pond ice. In Spring, the dams were blown open and the logs were flushed downstream in a rush of water. Here is an old dam site on Ampersand Brook.

## Some Stream Life

**Black Flies** are the single animal species that kept casual development out of the mountains for many decades. Its itchy swollen bites are caused by female flies needing blood protein for the development of their eggs.

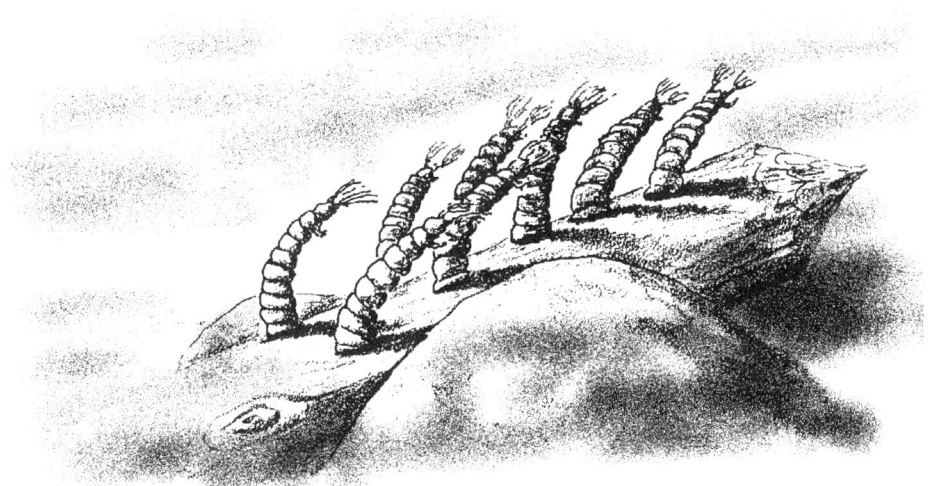

**Black Fly larva** coat rocks and sticks in well-oxygenated stream. The millions of larva begin to pupate when the water temperature reaches about 55 degrees F., which usually starts about mid-May. Adults emerge after a few days and hatching may continue well into July if the weather is cool and wet. A "white-legged" variety may hatch in September if unusually warm weather occurs.

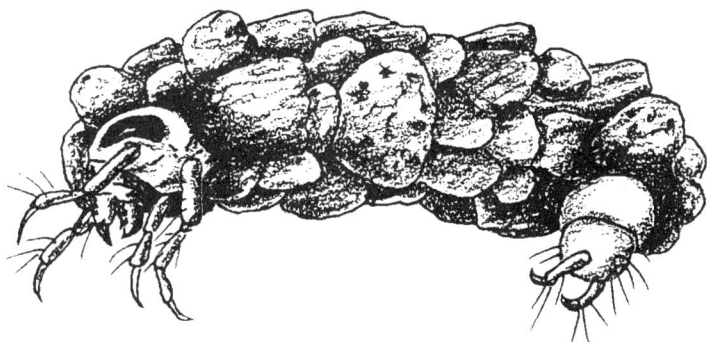

**Caddisfly larva** build protective cases around their bodies that camouflage these creatures. In fast-moving streams the cases are made of larger grains of sand that not only hide the animals, but also weigh them down to keep from being swept away.

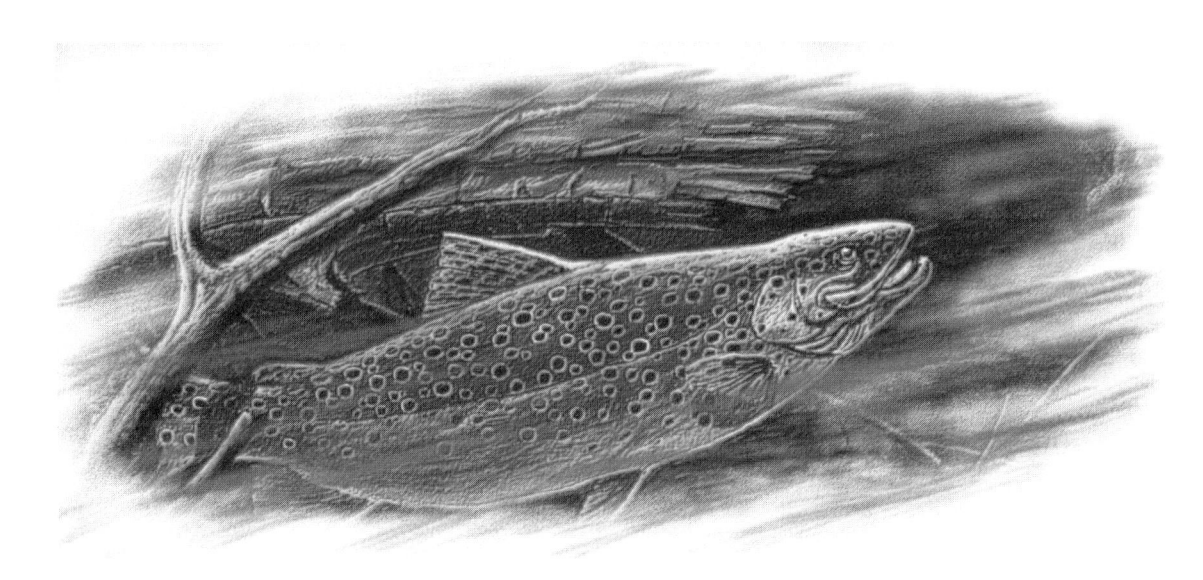

**Brown Trout** are European-native fish often stocked in larger rivers and ponds in the Adirondacks.

**Mink** are voracious stream feeders at the top of the food chain. They are secretive and curious animals that will investigate human intruders into their territories.

**Reading the Landscape** 131

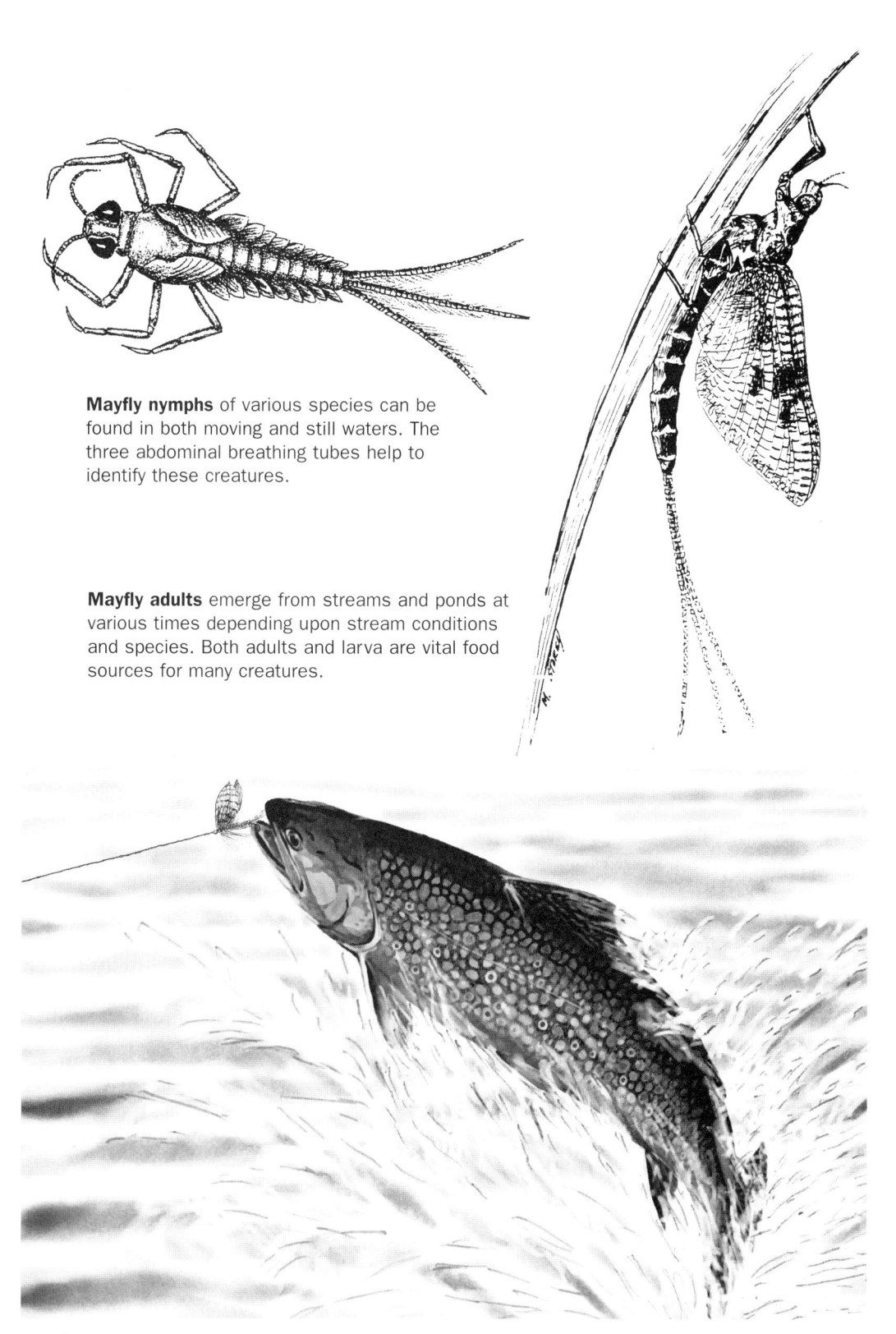

**Mayfly nymphs** of various species can be found in both moving and still waters. The three abdominal breathing tubes help to identify these creatures.

**Mayfly adults** emerge from streams and ponds at various times depending upon stream conditions and species. Both adults and larva are vital food sources for many creatures.

**Brook Trout** are the colorful native trout of the Adirondacks, and are sought by anglers in many kinds of habitats.

### Borne of Fire

The processes that heal wind-disturbed areas are nearly the same as those that heal forests hit by fire. Large forest fires rarely occur in the Adirondacks, but small blazes do pop up in dry summers. At the turn of the last century, huge fires erupted in the dry years of 1903, 1905 and 1908. In those three years alone, nearly one million acres burned in many areas of the Adirondacks. Most fires started near logging operations and the railroad lines that served them. Both hardwoods and softwoods were clearcut and hauled to mills by the trains. The tops of cut trees were left in huge brush piles along the way, and in dry years this tinderbox was easily ignited by locomotive sparks. Once a blaze began, only natural rainfall could put it out.

Fire behaves differently with different fuels. If an evergreen forest catches fire, the flames race through the crowns, exploding with great speed and intense heat. The duff, made up of slowly decaying needles, also burns with deep, searing heat. Wildfires there are slow to heal, and it may take centuries to revegetate to the original forest. Remember that evergreen forests usually occupy outwash sand and gravel soils or high mountain slopes, where soil nutrition is low. A classic example of a catastrophic fire in this situation is found several miles west of Paul Smiths, along the Blue Mountain Road. The sandy rolling plain is still largely a vast blueberry patch after nearly a century after the fires. The entire twenty-five miles of the gravel Blue Mountain Road passes through some of the wildest parts of the Park, much of it altered by fire. Bring your blueberry bucket if you go there in late summer.

Hardwood forests on till soils also burned in those years, but because these fires were often fairly light, they seldom killed the soil life. Wind-blown seeds of aspen and birch, as well as root suckers of damaged trees, quickly reforested the landscape. In the High Peaks and in many other places in the Park, you can find large areas of attractive paper birch forest, the natural healers of the land following fire. But these century-old

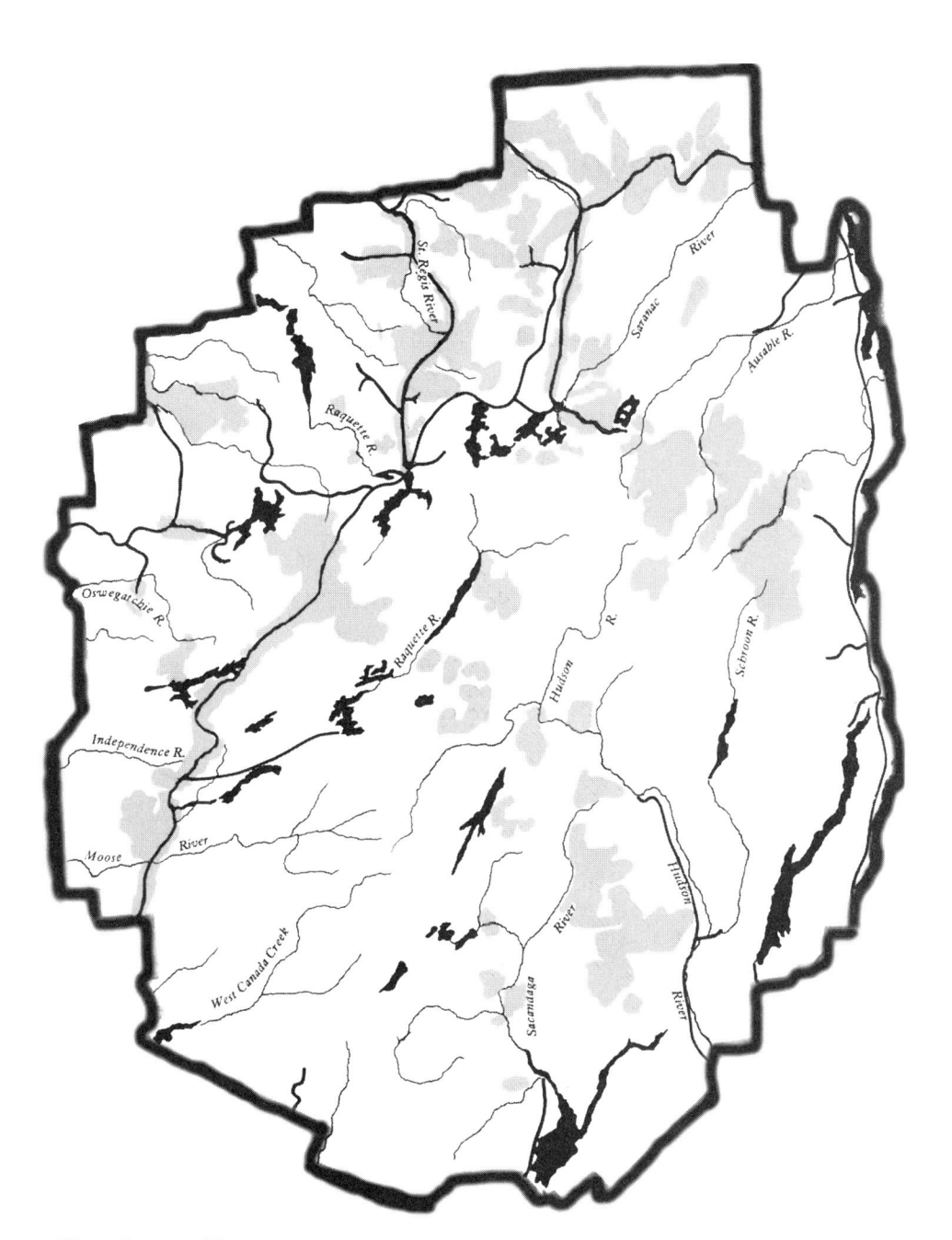

**More than a million acres** of Adirondack Forest burned in the years between 1900 and 1910. Heavy logging followed the railroads that snaked through the northwestern part of the new park. Fires started along these routes, where tons of dry tinder piled up. Major fire areas are marked in gray shade.

**134    Why the Adirondacks Look the Way They Do**

**Sandy outwash soils covered in evergreen forest** were especially vulnerable to deep hot fires. Here, along the Blue Mountain Road west of Paul Smiths, vast areas were burned. After more than a century, many places still have no forest cover and remain a vast blueberry patch.

forests are in a late-transition phase now, since the aspen and birch seldom live more than a hundred years, and other more long-lived and shade-tolerant species are starting to replace those "pioneer" forests. Red maple, yellow birch, sugar maple and balsam fir are beginning to form the future forests in these old burn areas. In the High Peaks, mountain paper birch is a variant of common paper birch, and it grows on burn areas all the way to many summits. Its leaves are more triangular than those of paper birch.

How can you tell for if you are in a fire disturbed area? First, look at the trees living there, and try to estimate their age. Aspen and paper birch are almost always present in burn areas. Also, look at the soil and pick around old stumps. You'll often find charcoal at the base of these old stumps, sometimes six inches or more deep in the humus (leaf litter). Charcoal is the pure carbon remains of the burn, and since no organism can consume or alter it, charcoal remains in the soil for centuries.

In dry summers, small forest fires are often sparked by careless brush burners or campers' untended fires. The eastern Adirondacks, including the Lake George and Champlain Valleys, are prone to more small fires than in the western Adirondacks because it is drier there and the oak- pine forests are easier to ignite. In the summer of 1989 a fire burned over 300

**Bigtooth Aspen**, here, as well as Quaking Aspen, have light wind-blown seeds that are carried long distances. They can settle into burn areas and germinate and grow quickly to heal a charred forest.

**Paper Birch** has light seeds that disperse throughout autumn and winter. Century-old birches are now mature and dying, being replaced by other species, such as these Balsam Firs.

### 136 Why the Adirondacks Look the Way They Do

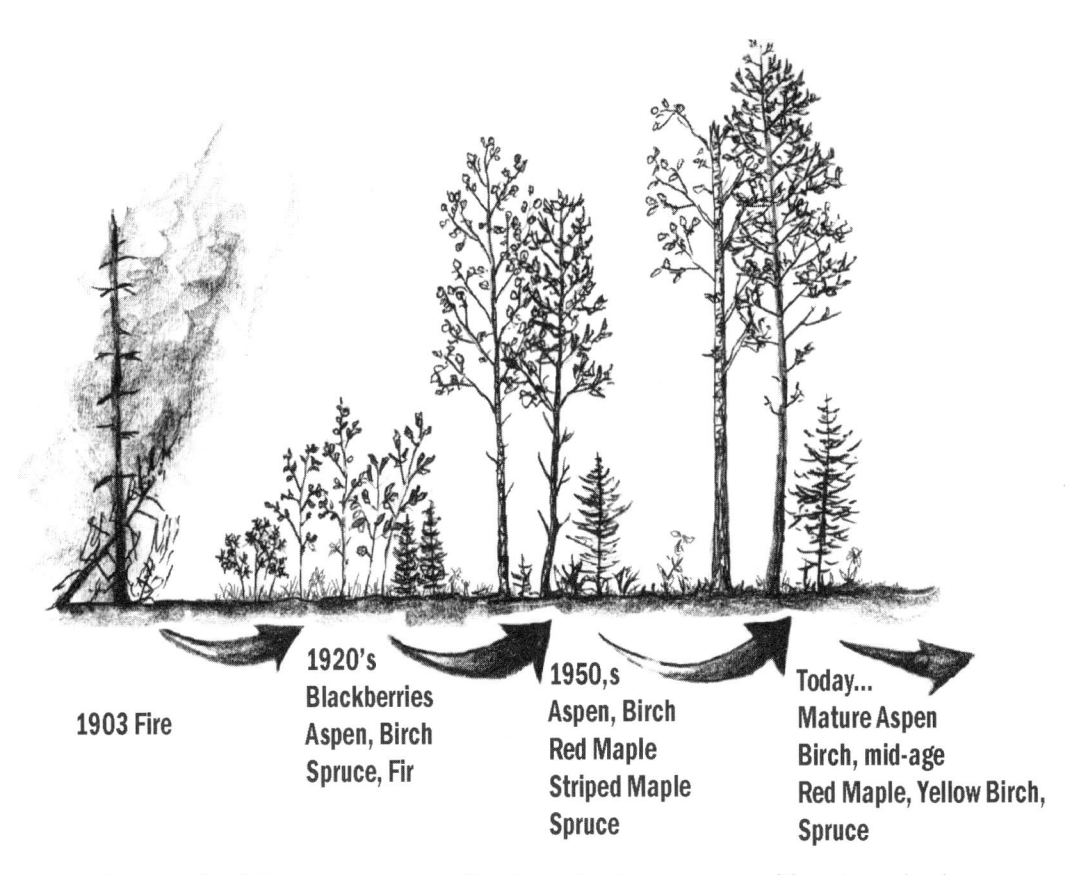

**Forest succession following a moderate fire.** A predictable sequence of forest species is evident in many places in the Park, as now seen in the High Peaks Wilderness Area.

1903 Fire → 1920's Blackberries, Aspen, Birch, Spruce, Fir → 1950,s Aspen, Birch, Red Maple, Striped Maple, Spruce → Today... Mature Aspen, Birch, mid-age Red Maple, Yellow Birch, Spruce

acres of second-growth forest near Vermontville, and the impact of that fire is evident today. A vigorous forest of young paper birch and aspen is rapidly reclaiming the spaces among the standing burned snags.

So, beavers, fire and windstorms shaped, and continue to shape, the Adirondack landscape. Windstorms will be the principal influence of the future, and fires will play a smaller role as time passes and the natural sequence of forest succession masks the big changes of the past century. Beavers will continue to influence the valley forests. Alterations in the living landscape are going on all the time, often so subtle that they go unrecognized. Several are worth mentioning, however, because they are molding the whole forest community of the future. They are acid rain and exotic plants and diseases.

## Reading the Landscape   137

**Lightning caused fires** are rare in the Adirondacks except for the Lake George-Lake Champlain areas of the Park. Here, a community of pine and oak dominates an area of dry conditions that favors summertime fires from ridge top lightning strikes.

**Here, a fire scare on an oak trunk** reveals evidence of an old burn near the summit of Shelving Rock Mountain on the east side of Lake George.

**Pitch Pine** is one of the few park communities based on fire. This three-needled pine has thick closed cones that only release seeds after being opened by a hot fire. The pine barrens communities perched on Lake Champlain's west shore highlands are found on sterile glacial sand delta deposits.

**The Vermontville fire** burned about 300 acres in second-growth fir and aspen in 1989. This photo was taken thirteen years after the fire, and shows a heavy regeneration of aspen and paper birch.

## Stories in the Snow

can be read during winter treks. Wildlife that is hidden in other times of the year often reveals its existence during a ski or snowshoe hike in the Adirondack forest. Even the most shy of animals become known by their sign and tracks.

**Meadow voles** have short tails and leave no tail drag marks in the snow. Winter migrants like **Rough-Legged Hawks** hunt these creatures in the open fields of the Adirondacks.

**Porcupines** stay active all winter and may be seen gnawing on bark in the same tree for weeks on end. They are very careful to conserve energy in cold weather.

# Reading the Landscape     139

**Snowshoe Hares** molt to a white coat in winter. The large hind feet have extra fur that acts as a snowshoe to lift the animal above the snow.

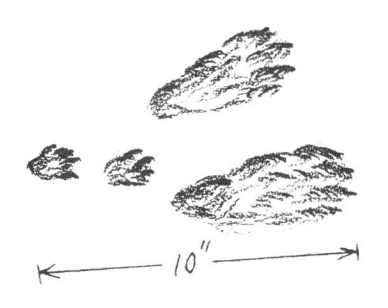

←— 10" —→

**Trekking the silent winter woods** on skis or snowshoes opens a world of hidden nature not seen in other seasons.

### 140    Why the Adirondacks Look the Way They Do

**Seldom seen in summer**, otters often scamper on the icy pond surface and surf the snow in playful glides.

**Both White-footed and Deer mice** run on the snow surface. They leave tail drag marks in the snow because they have long tails.

**Fishers** are secretive large members of the weasel family. They hunt porcupines, hares and red squirrels all winter and their tracks are more common than you would guess.

25"

# Reading the Landscape    141

**Both red and gray foxes** are common in the Adirondacks. Their tracks are smaller and usually in a tighter line compared to coyotes.

**White-tailed deer** are very common in the mountains. Their tracks can be seen throughout the year.

**A coyote-killed deer** found along the Esker Ski Trail at the Paul Smiths VIC. We found the animal shortly after it was taken, and it was fed upon by the coyote clan for three days before it was completely consumed. Only the hooves remained in the spring.

**Coyotes** are active in winter, hunting deer and other animals in small family packs, similar in behavior to wolves.

## Why the Adirondacks Look the Way They Do

**Dog tracks** tend to wander about, while foxes and coyotes stick to a determined route.

**Short-tailed weasels**, or ermine, molt to a winter white coat. These voracious hunters prey on mice, shrews. voles, chipmunks, and birds. On pure white snow, they look pale gold in color.

**Meadow voles** have short tails and leave no tail drag marks in the snow. Winter migrants like Rough-Legged Hawks hunt these creatures in the open fields of the Adirondacks.

**Ruffed Grouse** grow barbules on their toes that act like snowshoes on the snow surface. In very cold weather they will dive into soft snow to insulate their bodies. Both ruffed grouse and wild turkeys feed on buds of aspen and birch during the winter.

One of the diseases I have observed over the past forty years is beech-bark blight. This fungus was brought into North America from Europe at the turn of the twentieth century. Other exotic fungus diseases that have had devastating consequences on this continent include the chestnut blight and the Dutch elm disease. Trees evolving in North America have little or no defense against these exotic organisms, and easily succumb. The beech-bark disease spores are carried by tiny scale insects that are usually covered in a white wooly sheath. The insect penetrates the thin bark and sucks on the beech sap. While feeding, the insect inserts spores into the tree's plumbing system and the fungus begins to grow. Eventually the fungus invades the entire trunk just beneath the bark, and the fungal filaments girdle and kill the tree. The process may take anywhere from five to twenty five years. Other fungi, such as conks, may invade the tree as it weakens.

**The Beech-bark Blight** is transferred from one infected tree to another by a tiny scale insect hidden in a wooly coat, as seen in this photo. The insect pierces the bark and feeds on beech sap, and introduces the fungal spoors in the process.

**144**   **Why the Adirondacks Look the Way They Do**

**Beech Nuts**, the half-inch triangular fruits of the beech tree, are valuable food for many mammals and birds. The die-off of beech trees in the Adirondacks will have profound effects on most wildlife species here.

The death of beech trees has had an enormous effect on the Adirondack landscape and its wildlife. Beechnuts are the staple food for almost all non-predatory mammals in the Park. Mice, voles, chipmunks, squirrels, deer and bear all depend on beech nuts to fatten themselves before winter. Beeches are the only "nut" tree that is widespread and abundant in the central Adirondacks, so its demise is causing stress at all levels of the wildlife community. I'm not sure what alternative foods there are to take up the slack.

Beech is not a high-value hardwood like sugar maple and yellow birch, so beech trees were not logged. Beeches are versatile trees that compete well with other species on many kinds of soil and moisture conditions. As you hike through the forest, you will notice many large dead and dying beech trees. Look for the tiny wooly scale insects on the trunk and tiny garnet-colored club-like fruiting bodies of the fungus.

Also, notice that the dense undergrowth around dead beech trees is made up of hundreds of young root-sprouted beech trees. As a beech tree

**As the beech tree trunk dies**, it reacts by sending up root shoots to stay alive. This coppice of new trees surrounds the old trunk and forms a dense thicket. The new shoots usually acquire the fungus and perish before they can produce fruits.

dies, its still-healthy root system starts sending up leafy sprouts. The opening in the forest canopy created by the dead or dying top provides these young trees with a steady supply of solar energy, so they remain healthy for many decades. Eventually, as the sprouts age and get to sapling or pole size, they too become infected and the cycle starts again. These beech thickets are especially evident in midwinter, since the young treees hold their leaves which bleach out to an attractive bronze parchment color. The problem presented is the fact that the sprouts die before they become mature enough to produce beechnuts. So even though the life of the tree continues, wildlife suffer.

Acid rain is exacerbating the problem. Beech trees cycle calcium in their system, and in the Adirondacks calcium is in scarce supply. Calcium is one of the first elements to be leached from the soil by acid rain, and as this nutrient dwindles, beech trees become less able to withstand attacks of insect vectors and fungi. In calcium-rich areas of New York State, beech trees are in much better health.

Red spruce, one of the other premier forest trees of the Adirondacks, is also in trouble because of acid rain. Red Spruce depends upon fungal filaments attached to their roots to assist in the absorption of water and nutrients. Acid rain kills these helpful fungi, and the spruces slowly lose vigor and die. Red spruce occurs in just about all habitats in the Adirondacks: glacial outwash sands in valleys, as a component of northern hardwoods on glacial till, and on the upper slopes of mountains. As you hike in any of these areas you'll see many red spruce trees dead or dying. The upper spruce slopes of the High Peaks area have been particularly hard hit, with a majority of older trees now dead.

In 1984, I guided Noel Grove, an editor and writer for *National Geographic Magazine*, along with his photographer, on a flight over the High Peaks Wilderness Area. They were amazed and discouraged at the number of dead spruce covering the mountaintops and later wrote of their experience and published some of the photos they had gathered. Many of the dead trees were over two hundred years old and had survived the fires of 1903 and 1905, only to be done in by air pollution late in the century. In many of the first-growth hardwood forests where I have recently hiked in, I've seen dead spruces throughout the stand. Many trees exceeded three hundred years of age. The death of old trees in a forest is not an unusual thing, but the numbers of these dead giant red spruce that are now showing up in the forest is shocking.

Will it get better or worse? The federal Clean Air Act has worked to some degree, and some of the lakes and ponds in the Park have improved. Research has shown that sulfur dioxide levels have decreased

**Reading the Landscape   147**

**The die-off of red spruce trees** at higher elevations was first noted in the late 1970's. The problem was noted everywhere in the High Peaks area above 3500 feet, as here, south of Keene Valley.

**Old-growth Red Spruce** trees are now dying at the lower elevations throughout the park. This 300 year-old giant was photographed in the trail to Raquette Falls.

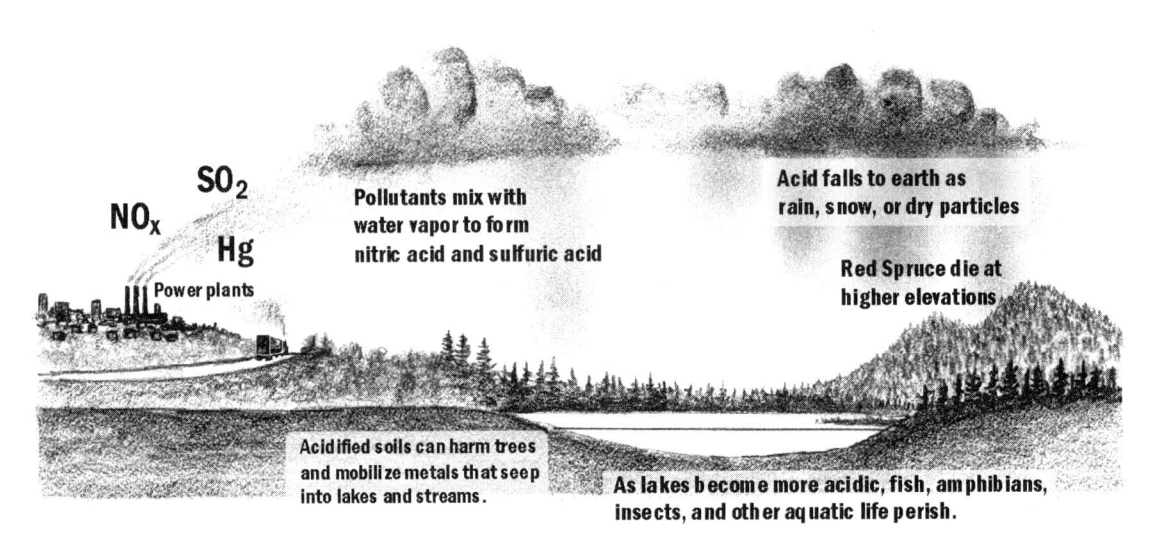

**Acid Rain** falls everywhere in eastern North America. Many areas like the Adirondacks have little buffering in soils to neutralize the acidity that falls from the sky, so a lethal buildup attacks all levels of life on land and in the water.

somewhat, but that nitrogen oxides have remained about the same. Automobile exhaust is a major source of pollutants, and older coal-fired power plants continue to pour out the deadly precursors of acid rain, as well as substantial amounts of mercury that harm life. Vigilance of federal air pollution laws and the strengthening of existing laws will help solve this pervasive Adirondack problem. Nature has a tremendous ability to bounce back if given the opportunity as long as the basic structure of the ecological community remains intact. The Adirondacks certainly retain the capability to recover.

### People Choose

The people of New York State can take the credit for allowing nature to bring the Adirondacks back to its wild condition. The Forest Preserve was created in 1885, by a law that stipulated that all state-owned land in the Adirondack and Catskill counties would be preserved as wild forest land and that no timber cutting would be allowed. The Adirondack Park was created in 1892 as the region where state land ownership should concentrate. An amendment was added to the state constitution in 1894 that gave ironclad protection to the Forest Preserve.

In 1972, the state created the Adirondack Park Agency (APA). The two plans that it administers, one for private land and one for state land, help to control development and focus management that protects the entire landscape. But, since both the APA and the Department of Environmental Conservation (DEC) are political in nature, citizen watchdogging is always necessary.

Over the years, battles by individuals were fought and won that further protected the forest and waters of the Adirondack Park. Robert Marshall, scaler of the forty-six highest Adirondack peaks and resident of the Park, organized the Wilderness Society, which encourages the creation and management of wilderness areas in the United States and throughout the world. Proposals to build dams on many of the Park's free-flowing rivers were defeated by Paul Schaefer and members of the Association for the Protection of the Adirondacks over many years. The Adirondack Nature Conservancy has bought and preserved thousands of acres in the Adirondacks, much of it open to public use, education and enjoyment.

**Eurasian Milfoil** is now found in almost every large lake and pond accessible to boats, carried by careless boaters from one water body to another.

# Why the Adirondacks Look the Way They Do

**All moose** were tagged and followed as they returned to the Adirondacks in the early 1980's. It was a pleasant surprise to wildlife biologists that they survived so well in competition with deer and people. Photo by Joe Martens.

**Ravens** returned in the mid-1960's and are now common throughout the Adirondacks

**Mountain Lions** are surely here, with dozens of sightings every year in the Adirondacks. Whether they are native returnees or escaped pets, only future testing will tell.

**Timber Rattlesnakes** are found in the Lake George-Lake Champlain Valleys. These secretive animals appear to have a stable population.

**Wild Turkeys** have learned to use the tactics of grouse, feeding on buds during the winter when other foods are buried under snow and ice.

# Reading the Landscape    151

**The Peregrine Falcon** was brought back in the early 1980's and small numbers are seen throughout the state.

**Moose numbers** were estimated at about 250 in 2006, and with a mix of males and females about even, the population is expected to grow rapidly.

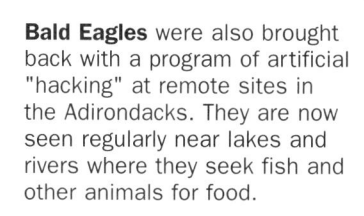

**Bald Eagles** were also brought back with a program of artificial "hacking" at remote sites in the Adirondacks. They are now seen regularly near lakes and rivers where they seek fish and other animals for food.

**Gray Wolves** may be in the Adirondacks right now (2006). Sightings by many people and recognizable tracks indicate their presence. These animals easily coexist with humans and other wildlife, but the coyote population may be reduced by wolf competition.

### 152 Why the Adirondacks Look the Way They Do

**A single white house** on a hillside can destroy the pristine view of an entire valley.

We continue to need vigilance and action when new onslaughts arise. Acid rain and other air pollutants, like mercury and ozone, create a particularly sneaky and pervasive deadly force that needs federal attention, since much of the problem comes from outside the borders of New York.

Motorized vehicles such as ATV's and jet skis destroy the solitude as well as damage the environment. Development of ridges and mountainsides is another disturbing development trend. One trophy house on a slope can spoil an entire vista.

The old adage, "Nature knows best" should continue to guide our management of the Adirondacks. The Park is wild because the people of New York have let nature take its course, all for the better. My guess is that along with moose and wild turkeys, we may soon have wolves and mountain lions here also to share in the beautiful wildness that exemplifies this great park. Keep a focused eye on why the Adirondacks look the way they do and join in their future protection.

**Help protect this great Adirondack Park** by keeping a sharp eye on its health and what may help or harm it in the future.

**154    Why the Adirondacks Look the Way They Do**

# Glossary of Ecological Terms

**Abiotic:** a non-living factor in an environment, e.g., light, water, minerals, temperature.

**Adaptation:** a genetic or behavioral trait or pattern that enhances an organism's ability to survive and reproduce in its environment.

**Animal community:** animals of various species living within a certain habitat, each occupying its own niche; directly parallel and related to plant communities.

**Aquatic:** living or growing in freshwater, as compared to *marine* in salt water.

**Biotic community:** commonly the living organisms in a given community. The non-living parts are considered the abiotic.

**Bog:** a wetland formed by glacial melting where surface drainage is congested. Low oxygen, pH, and water temperature cause incomplete decomposition, resulting in the buildup of fibrous peat. Only specialized organisms can colonize these extreme conditions, such as pitcher plants, orchids and sphagnum moss. A **fen** is a bog like system in which more surface water flows through, thus allowing more oxygen and nutrients to be available to organisms. Fens are more common in the Adirondacks than classic kettle-hole bogs.

**Browse:** to eat twigs, bark and buds of woody plants, especially in winter. Deer and moose are browsers in winter when more nutritious live green plants are unavailable.

**Carnivore:** any chiefly flesh-eating mammal, usually in the dog, cat or weasel family.

**Carrying capacity:** a wildlife-management term for the total number of any species that a given area of habitat will support at any given time; the ability of a given unit of habitat to supply food, water, shelter and escape cover as well as the territorial space necessary to a wildlife species; the number and quality of organisms of a given species that can survive in a given ecosystem without causing deterioration; the largest population any unit can support on a year-round basis, or during the most critical time of the year, and from year to year, depending upon conditions within the habitat such as rainfall, competition, temperature and snowfall. In the Adirondacks, winters with extreme snowfall and low temperatures strongly influence carrying capacity of the larger mammals.

**Climax community:** the final stage in ecological succession that is relatively stable and during which plants and animals are capable of reproducing in the environment they helped to create. Climax communities can be altered by disruptions such as windstorms, disease outbreaks, fire or human activity.

**Community:** an association of organisms—plant and animal—each occupying a certain position or ecological niche, inhabiting a common environment, and interacting with each other; all the plants and animals in a particular habitat that are bound together by food chains and other interrelationships. In the Adirondacks, the Northern hardwood forest is the major community that covers the landscape.

**Competition:** when two or more organisms have the potential for using the same resource.

**Coniferous:** refers to cone-bearing trees. A coniferous forest is composed of various pines, firs, spruces cedars or hemlocks. Coniferous forests usually occupy low-nutrient soils.

**Conservation:** the wise use of natural resources in a way that assures their continuing healthy availability to future generations; the wise use or preservation of natural resources.

**Consumers:** organisms that cannot make their own food and must obtain energy by eating other living things.

**Cover:** the vegetation, debris and irregularities of the land or water that provide concealment, sleeping, feeding and breeding areas for wildlife.

**Crepuscular:** active at dusk and dawn. Many Adirondack animals are crepuscular in nature.

**Decomposers:** organisms (such as bacteria and fungi) that break down plant and animal remains into forms once again usable by producers.

**Deep water habitat:** aquatic habitats where water is deeper than 2 meters (6.6 feet), the deepest water in which rooted emergent plants can survive, such as water lilies, water shield and pickerelweed.

**Dispersal:** the movement of organisms into new habitats and locations. Dispersal can occur via adults, juveniles or young in animals, or via the transport (by wind, water, animals or other means) of specialized structures such as seeds, spores, eggs and cysts.

**Diurnal:** of the daytime or occurring during daylight hours.

**Diversity:** the variety, number and distribution of species in a community.

**Ecology:** the study of the relation of organisms to their environment; the science of the interrelations between organisms and their environment.

**Ecosystem:** a natural unit that includes living and nonliving parts interacting to produce a stable system with a closed exchange of materials between the living and nonliving parts.

**Ecotone:** the juncture of two or more kinds of habitats, such as the edge between a marsh and a forest. Landscapes with many ecotones produce the greatest ecological diversity.

**Environment:** all of the surroundings—air, water, vegetation, human elements, wildlife—that has influence on you and your existence.

**Ethics:** a personal or social moral code.

**Eutrophic:** referring to a body of water, high in organic matter and mineral nutrients (e.g., phosphate and nitrate) and often exhibiting seasonal oxygen deficiency. Oligotrophic refers to waterbodies with a low-nutrient watershed exhibiting clear water.

**Filter feeder:** organisms that feed by sieving fine particles from water, such as clams and black fly larva.

**Food chain:** the transfer of food energy from the plant source through a series of animals, with repeated eating and being eaten, such as a green plant > leaf-eating insect > insect-eating bird > hawk.

**Forest:** a complex community of plant layers and various organisms and animals in which trees are the dominant members.

**Habitat:** the arrangement of food, water, shelter or cover and space suitable to animal needs. It is the "life range" which must include food and water, as well as escape cover, winter cover and safe places to raise young.

**Herb layer:** the soft-stemmed plants close to the forest floor.

**Lacustrine:** referring to lakes.

**Limiting factors:** influences in the life history of any animal, population of animals, or species; e.g., food, water, shelter, space, disease, predation, severe weather, pollution and accidents. When one or more of these exceeds the limit of tolerance of an animal or population, then it becomes a limiting factor. Limiting factors may result from natural or human-caused events.

**Littoral:** the shoreline zone of a lake where sunlight penetrates to the bottom and is sufficient to support rooted plant growth.

**Lotic:** of flowing water.

**Marsh (freshwater):** a wetland where standing water exists year-round, except in the shallower areas during late summer of unusually dry years. The deep-water limit occurs where water depth exceeds two meters. Marshes man support the growth of emergent plants such as cattails, rushes, reeds, sedges, pickerelweeds; floating-leaved plants like waterlilies and watershield; floating plants such as duckweed and submergents like water lettuce. Soil may be sand, silt or soft black muck.

**Mast:** nuts or large seeds, such as oak, beech and black cherry, that are important food sources for many bird and mammals.

**Microhabitat:** a small habitat within a larger one, such as a hole in a tree trunk or an animal carcass on the forest floor.

**Migration:** the periodic movement of animals from one area to another. Plants also can migrate with climatic change, such as after the ice age 13,000 years ago.

**Natural selection:** a process in nature that favors the survival and perpetuation of organisms whose characteristics enable them to adapt best to their environment.

## Glossary of Ecological Terms

**Neuston:** the community of organisms that live on top of, or suspended from, the surface film of water, such as a water strider or mosquito larva.

**Niche:** the ecological role or position that a living thing or group occupies in an ecosystem. A fungus, for example, occupies the niche of a decomposer that breaks down a dead plant or animal.

**Omnivore:** an animal that eats several kinds of food, possibly including plants, animals and detritus. Herbivores are animals that eat just plants.

**Organic matter:** chemical components of carbon combined with other chemical elements, and generally manufactured in the life processes of plants and animals. Most organic components are a source of food for bacteria and are usually combustible.

**Peat:** organic matter composed of fibrous, spongy, partially decomposed plants. Peat forms under conditions where decomposition is incomplete, such as in a bog, where oxygen is low and a floating mat of sphagnum moss supplies the raw materials.

**Predation:** an action during which one organism (predator) kills and eats another (prey).

**Producer:** green plants that are capable of changing inorganic elements into organic tissue, such as the action of chlorophyll in combination with sunlight to combine water and carbon dioxide into sugar molecules.

**Resident wildlife:** animals that occupy a region or habitat on a year-round basis, and do not migrate.

**Scavenger:** any animal that eats dead organic matter. Some beetles, ravens and crows, coyotes, blue jays, chickadees, and some butterflies fall into this category.

**Sere:** a stage in a predictable series of communities that follow one another in a natural succession, as in the change from bare ground to a field to a forest.

**Snag:** a standing dead tree from which leaves and most branches have fallen; important as a wildlife nesting and resting place. In the Adirondacks snags are often created by beavers flooding valley forests killing trees in a matter of months.

**Stewardship:** the concept of responsible care-taking, based on the premise that we do not own resources or land, but are managers of those things and are responsible to future generations for their condition.

**Stress:** usually thought of as a physical factor that applies detrimental pressure to an organism or population. A drought would apply stress to a plant community and thereby to an animal population, and this would perhaps inhibit reproduction rather than eliminate a species.

**Succession:** the orderly, gradual and continuous replacement of one plant and animal community by another.

**Swamp:** a wetland with woody vegetation as the dominant plant that is periodically flooded with water. In the Adirondacks, swamps can be composed of either hardwoods or conifer trees, such as silver maple, white cedar, tamarack or black spruce.

**Territory:** the concept of "ownership" or dominance over a unit of habitat; an area defended by an animal against others of the same species; used for breeding, feeding or both. Most species of mammals and birds are strongly territorial and claim and hold space for each breeding cycle.

**Understory:** the layer of plants growing under a higher layer of plants, e.g., herbs and shrubs under forest trees.

**Wild:** not tamed or domesticated, living in a basically free condition. A wild animal provides for its own food, shelter and other needs in an environment that serves as a suitable habitat.

**Yard (deer):** a sheltered area in winter when general snow depth exceeds 18 inches; especially applied to white-tailed deer in coniferous swamps in the Adirondacks.

# Index

1950 Windstorm  115
Acid rain  146
**Acid rain diagram**  148
**Adirondack Lake Country**  41
**Adirondack Park**  1
**Adirondack Rocks**  7
**Alien plants**  91
Anorthosite  12
**Anorthosite Road Cut**  13
Appalachian Range  22
Atlantic Ocean  22
**AuSable Chasm**  20
Ausable Point marsh  77
**Balsam Fir Cones**  96
**Barton Garnet Mine**  12
Bat hibernation  11
Beaver Lodge cross-section  112
Beavers  103
**Beech coppice**  145
**Beech nuts**  144
**Beech-bark blight**  143
**Bicknell's Thrush**  90
**Bigtooth Aspen**  135
**Birds of Summer**  100-101
**Birds planting**  125-127
**Black Spruce**  65
**Blue Mountain Lake**  26
**Blue Mt. Road fires**  134
**Bog Cross-section**  47
Bogs  77
**Bogs and Boreal Life**  78-81
**Boreal Birds**  82-83
**Boreal Life Trail**  76
**Brook life**  86
**Canadian Shield**  3
Champ sea monster  53
Champlain Valley  53
**Champlain Valley birds**  84
**Cirques, Giant Mountain**  52
**Cirques, Whiteface**  51
Clay, marine  60
**Crane Mountain**  28
**Dams**  128
**Drainage Pattern**  27
Earthquakes  29
Eldon Lake  48
**Elm, American**  64
**Eskers**  44-45
**Eurasian Milfoil**  149
**Exfoliation Dome**  16
Fire scar  137
**Fishing Brook dam**  98

**Foam on streams**  97
**Forest Fire map**  133
**Forest Fire Succession**  136
Forest fires  132
Forest on the Wing  123
Garnet  11
**Geology Map**  6
**Geology Timeline**  8
Glacial erratics  38-39
**Glacial Features formation**  44
**Glossary of Terms**  155-159
**Gneiss and Marble bands**  14
Graben  18
**Graben**  19
Granitic gneiss  16
**Gravel deposit**  57
Grenville Orogeny  4
**Hardwoods, old-growth**  89
**Hay-scented ferns**  99
**Hemlock illust**  88
**Hemlocks, old-growth**  87
**Hot Spot**  23
**Ice plucking**  40
**Ice Sheet Lobes**  35
**Indian Lake**  19
Isostatic rebound  52
**Jenkins Mountain Esker**  45
John Brown's Farm  43
**Kettle Hole**  46
**Kettle Lake formation**  46
Kunjamuk River  28
Lake George glaciation  37
**Lake Tear**  26
**Lampson's Falls**  29
Land bridge  54
**Life Zones diagram**  93
**Limestone exposure**  23
**Loess Deposits**  61
Loess soil  60
**Long Lake blowdown**  120
**Magnetite Sand**  10
Marble  14
**Marble Road Cut**  15
Mariah (wind)  113
Marsh  68
**Marsh life illustrations**  70-75
**Massawepie Esker**  50
Middle Saranac Beach  48
**Middle Saranac Beach**  51
**Natural Stone Bridge**  15
**Newcomb VIC Beavers**  108
Olympic ski jumps  43

Pan layer  62
**Paper Birch**  135
**Pitch Pine**  137
Pitted outwash plain  47
Pleistocene Era  35
**Radial Drainage**  24
**Rainbow Lake Esker**  45
Reading the Landscape  103
**Red Oak**  65
**Red Pines**  96
**Red Spruce**  65
**Red Spruce, dead**  147
**Relief Map**  31
**Returning Wildlife**  150-151
**Saint Regis Canoe Area**  48
Salt water sea  53
**Sand Barrens Community**  53
Saranac River  30
Saratoga Springs  22
**Shoreline ridges**  123
**Silver Lake Mountain**  40
**Silver Maple**  66
**Snow fleas**  56
**Soil organisms**  54
**Soil Profile**  58
Soils  54
**Springtails**  56
**Stilt trees**  121
**Stories in the Snow**  138-142
**Stream life illust.**  129-131
**Sub-alpine zone**  91
**Sugar Maple**  60
Swamp  68
**Sweetfern**  92
**Tahawas Mine**  9
Till soil  60
**Tilted yellow birch**  117
**Tree Pollen Time Line**  67
**Trees in Tough Places**  120-121
Trellis drainage pattern  27
**Trilliums**  64
Trilobite  21
**Trophy House**  152
**Tupper Lake wetland**  76
Waterfalls  29
**White Cedars**  94-95
**White Pines**  63
**Windstorms Map**  118
**Windthrow illustrations**  114
Wisconsin period  36

## About the Author

Mike Storey grew up in Hamburg, New York, a rural suburb of Buffalo. He loved hunting and fishing and exploring nature in the fields and forests around his home. He received a BS degree (1966) and MS degree (1977) from the SUNY College of Environmental Science and Forestry at Syracuse University. He was art editor of the college's yearbook, *Empire Forester*, in 1965.

During the summers of 1965 and 1966, he was a seasonal ranger-naturalist at Old Faithful in Yellowstone National Park. He married his wife, Joan, in Bozeman, Montana in 1966. Mike became a full-time Park Service naturalist, and was sent to Grand Canyon National Park for federal service ranger school training. He was then stationed at Flamingo, in Everglades National Park, Florida, as acting district naturalist.

He returned to New York for graduate school and in 1970 was later hired as the naturalist, and eventually the director, of Beaver Lake Nature Center in Baldwinsville, NY, where he designed the trails and education programs. While there, he published his first book, *Heartland, a Natural History of Onondaga County, NY.*

Mike became the Park Naturalist for the Adirondack Park Agency in 1977 and began organizing education programs for Adirondack schools. He was the project leader in the development of a 250 page Environmental Education Resource Manual for Adirondack Schools, produced jointly with the Dept. of Environmental Conservation. In 1984 he instigated the development of a visitor contact system in the Adirondack Park and was instrumental in the selection and development of the two centers at Newcomb and Paul Smiths. He designed the trail systems and interpretation at both centers. During his years at the Park Agency, he taught thousands of students and conducted dozens of teacher training workshops and slide programs

He retired in 2001 and currently operates an interpretive design consulting business for nature-related facilities in the Northeast, as well as doing the wildlife illustrations for the *Adirondack Explorer* Magazine. He vigorously supports political action that preserves the commons of clean air, water and land that sustain life in this beautiful country.